A RUMI ANTHOLOGY

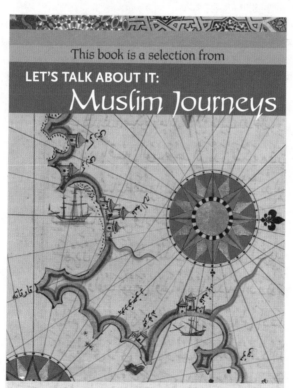

This book is a selection from

LET'S TALK ABOUT IT:
Muslim Journeys

bridgingcultures.neh.gov/muslimjourneys

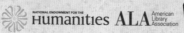

OTHER TITLES IN THIS SERIES

Flatland, Edwin A. Abbott, ISBN 1–85168–086–1

RELATED TITLES PUBLISHED BY ONEWORLD

City of Wrong, translated by Kenneth Cragg, ISBN 1–85168–072–1

Rumi: Past and Present, East and West, Franklin D. Lewis,
  ISBN 1–85168–214–7

The Practice of the Presence of God, Brother Lawrence,
  ISBN 1–85168–198–1

Rumi: A Spiritual Treasury, compiled by Juliet Mabey,
  ISBN 1–85168–215–5

Concerning the Inner Life, Evelyn Underhill, ISBN 1–85168–194–9

The Essentials of Mysticism, Evelyn Underhill, ISBN 1–85168–195–7

Mysticism, Evelyn Underhill, ISBN 1–85168–196–0

The Spiritual Life, Evelyn Underhill, ISBN 1–85168–197–3

A RUMI ANTHOLOGY

RUMI: POET AND MYSTIC
TALES OF MYSTIC MEANING

TRANSLATED BY
REYNOLD A. NICHOLSON

ONEWORLD
OXFORD

A RUMI ANTHOLOGY

Oneworld Publications
(Sales and Editorial)
185 Banbury Road
Oxford OX2 7AR
England
http://www.oneworld-publications.com

ISBN 1–85168–251–1

Cover design by Design Deluxe, Bath
Printed and bound in Great Britain by Creative Print and
Design

RUMI: POET AND MYSTIC

CONTENTS

11

INTRODUCTION

I

JALĀLU'L-DĪN RŪMĪ, the greatest mystical poet of Persia, was born at Balkh in the northern Persian province of Khorasan in A.D. 1207. The city at that time flourished under the rule of Muḥammad, the great Shah of Khwarizm, whose empire, as E. G. Browne described it, "extended from the Ural Mountains to the Persian Gulf, and from the Indus almost to the Euphrates." The family to which our poet belonged had been settled in Balkh for several generations; it was highly respected and, according to his biographers, had produced a notable succession of jurists and divines. So far as can be ascertained, its history begins with his great-grandfather, who claimed descent from Arab stock, and from no less a person than Abū Bakr, the first Caliph of Islam.

Although the Eastern biographies of Rūmī, like other lives of Persian saints, are to a large extent legendary, while his own works characteristically contribute virtually nothing in the shape of historical facts, we are fortunate in possessing some old and relatively trustworthy sources of information.[1] The following sketch, based on the chief materials available, gives briefly the main circumstances of Rūmī's life and describes some of the events which were the source of his mystical enthusiasm and poetic inspiration.

In 1219, when Jalālu'l-Dīn was twelve years old, his father, Bahā'u'l-Dīn Walad, suddenly departed from Balkh with his family and journeyed westward. The motives

[1] See Note, p.27.

17

alleged for this migration, that it was the result either of divine inspiration or human intrigue, are surely fictitious. There can be no doubt that Bahā'u'l-Dīn, like many thousands of others, fled before the terrible Mongol hordes, which were sweeping through Khorasan and already approaching his native city. News of its devastation reached the exiles on their way to Baghdad or on the next stage of their long journey from Baghdad to Mecca, when they travelled to Damascus and finally settled in Rum (Turkey).

Their first home was at Zarandah, about forty miles south-east of Konia, where Jalālu'l-Dīn married; in 1226 his eldest son Sultān Walad was born. Presently Bahā'u'l-Dīn transferred himself and his family to Konia, at that time the capital of the Western Seljuk empire, and he died there in 1230. He is said to have been an eminent theologian, a great teacher and preacher, venerated by his pupils and highly esteemed by the reigning monarch, to whom he acted as a spiritual guide. About this time Burhānu'l-Dīn Muḥaqqiq of Tirmidh, a former pupil of Bahā'u'l-Dīn at Balkh, arrived in Konia. Under his influence, it is said, Jalālu'l-Dīn, now in his twenty-fifth year, became imbued with enthusiasm for the discipline and doctrine of the Ṣūfīs—men and women who sought to unite themselves with God. During the next decade he devoted himself to imitation of his Pīr and passed through all the stages of the mystical life until, on the death of Burhānu'l-Dīn in 1240, he in turn assumed the rank of Shaykh and thus took the first, though probably unpremeditated, step towards forming a fraternity of the disciples whom his ardent personality attracted in ever increasing numbers.

The remainder of his life, as described by his son, falls into three periods, each of which is marked by a mystical intimacy of the closest kind with a "Perfect Man," i.e. one of the saints in whom Divine attributes are mirrored, so that the lover, seeing himself by the light of God, realizes that he and his Beloved are not two, but One. These

18

experiences lie at the very centre of Rūmī's theosophy and directly or indirectly inspire all his poetry. In handling the verse narrative of a mystic's son who was himself a mystic it is prudent to make ample allowance for the element of allegory; yet it would be rash to reject the whole story as pious fiction seeing that at the date when it was written many persons were living who could say whether it was, or was not, a recognizable picture of things which they themselves had witnessed.

In 1244 a wandering dervish, known to posterity by the name of Shamsu'l-Dīn of Tabriz, arrived at Konia. Jalālu'l-Dīn found in the stranger that perfect image of the Divine Beloved which he had long been seeking. He took him away to his house, and for a year or two they remained inseparable. Sultān Walad likens his father's all-absorbing communion with this "hidden saint" to the celebrated journey of Moses in company with Khaḍir (Koran, xviii, 64–80), the Sage whom Ṣūfīs regard as the supreme hierophant and guide of travellers on the Way to God. Meanwhile the Maulawī (Mevlevi)[1] disciples of Rūmī, entirely cut off from their Master's teaching and conversation and bitterly resenting his continued devotion to Shamsu'l-Dīn alone, assailed the intruder with abuse and threats of violence. At last Shamsu'l-Dīn fled to Damascus, but was brought back in triumph by Sultān Walad, whom Jalālu'l-Dīn, deeply agitated by the loss of his bosom friend, had sent in search of him. Thereupon the disciples "repented" and were forgiven. Soon, however, a renewed outburst of jealousy on their part caused Shamsu'l-Dīn to take refuge in Damascus for the second time, and again Sultān Walad was called upon to restore the situation. Finally, perhaps in 1247, the man of mystery vanished without leaving a trace behind.

[1] The title for Rūmī's followers; Rūmī was known among them as *Maulānā* ("Our Master"). Mevlevi is the Turkish pronunciation of Maulawī.

Sulṭān Walad vividly describes the passionate and uncontrollable emotion which overwhelmed his father at this time.

> "Never for a moment did he cease from listening to
>   music (samāʿ), and dancing;
> Never did he rest by day or night.
> He had been a mufti: he became a poet;
> He had been an ascetic: he became intoxicated by
>   Love.
> 'Twas not the wine of the grape: the illumined soul
>   drinks only the wine of Light."

Here Sulṭān Walad alludes to the *Dīwān-i Shams-i Tabrīz* ("Lyrics of Shams of Tabriz"), an immense collection of mystical odes composed by Jalālu'l-Dīn in the name of Shamsu'l-Dīn and dedicated to the memory of his *alter ego*. The first verse does not confirm, but may have suggested, the statement of some authorities that grief for the loss of Shams-i Tabrīz caused Jalālu'l-Dīn to institute the characteristic Mevlevi religious dance with its plaintive reed-flute accompaniment.

The next episode (*circa* 1252–1261) in Jalālu'l-Dīn's spiritual life is a fainter repetition of the last. For many years after the disappearance of Shamsu'l-Dīn he devoted himself to Ṣalāḥu'l-Dīn Farīdūn Zarkūb, who as his deputy (*khalīfah*) was charged with the duty of instructing the Mevlevi acolytes. They showed their resentment in no uncertain manner, and the ringleaders only gave in when they had been virtually excommunicated.

On the death of Ṣalāḥu'l-Dīn (*circa* 1261) the poet's enthusiasm found a new and abundant source of inspiration in another disciple, Ḥusāmu'l-Dīn Ḥasan ibn Muḥammad ibn Ḥasan ibn Akhī Turk, whose name he has mystically associated with his greatest work, the celebrated *Mathnawī* (epic poem). He calls the *Mathnawī* "the book of Ḥusām" and likens himself to a flute on the lips of Ḥusāmu'l-Dīn,

20

pouring forth "the wailful music that he made." During the last ten years of the poet's life this last beloved follower acted as his *khalīfah*, and upon his death in 1273 succeeded him as Head of the Mevlevi Order, a dignity he held until 1284, when Sulṭān Walad took his place.

To this first-hand account of Rūmī's life given in verse by his son the later prose biographers add little that can be considered either important or trustworthy. From Aflākī and others we hear that he was guide, philosopher and friend, not only to the Seljuk minister Mu'īnu'l-Dīn, the Parwānah (Governor) of Rum, but to his royal master, Sulṭān 'Alā'u'l-Dīn himself; in any case it would seem that he and the group of Ṣūfīs around him enjoyed influential support and were in a position to defy attacks on their doctrine. The poet takes a high line with his orthodox critics. He calls them "boobies" and "curs baying at the moon."

A Platonic type of mystical love had been cultivated by Ṣūfīs long before Rūmī declared that he and Shams-i Tabrīz were "two bodies with one soul." In this union of loving souls all distinctions vanish: nothing remains but the essential Unity of Love, in which "lover" and "beloved" have merged their separate identities. In calling his lyrics the *Dīwān* (Poems) of Shams-i Tabrīz, Rūmī of course uses the name Shams as though Shams and himself had become identical and were the same person. Though to us Shams's figure may appear unsubstantial, we need not accept the view put forward by some modern scholars that he is merely a personification of Jalālu'l-Dīn's poetic and mystical genius—an Eastern equivalent for "the Muse." Those who adopt that theory must logically extend it to include Ṣalāḥu'l-Dīn and Ḥusāmu'l-Dīn and can hardly avoid the implication that Sulṭān Walad created three imaginary characters to play the leading parts in his father's life and in the foundation of the Mevlevi Order. Western students of the *Dīwān* and the *Mathnawi* will recall a celebrated parallel that points the other way. Did not Dante transfigure the *donna gentil* who was the object of his romantic passion into Celestial Wisdom and glorify her under the name of Beatrice?

II

Rūmī's literary output, as stupendous in magnitude as it is sublime in content, consists of the very large collection of mystical odes, perhaps as many as 2,500, which make up the *Dīwān-i Shams-i Tabrīz*; the *Mathnawī* in six books of about 25,000 rhyming couplets; and the *Rubā'īyat* or quatrains, of which maybe about 1,600 are authentic.[1] The forms in which he clothes his religious philosophy had been fashioned before him by two great Ṣūfī poets, Sanā'ī of Ghaznah and Farīdu'l-Dīn 'Aṭṭār of Nishapur. Though he makes no secret of his debt to them both, his flight takes a wider range, his materials are richer and more varied, and his method of handling the subject is so original that it may justly be described as "a new style." It is a style of great subtlety and complexity, hard to analyse; yet its general features are simple and cannot be doubted. In the *Mathnawī*, where it is fully developed, it gives the reader an exhilarating sense of largeness and freedom by its disregard for logical cohesion, defiance of conventions, bold use of the language of common life, and abundance of images drawn from homely things and incidents familiar to every one. The poem resembles a trackless ocean: there are no boundaries; no lines of demarcation between the literal "husk" and the "kernel" of doctrine in which its inner sense is conveyed and copiously expounded. The effortless fusion of text and interpretation shows how completely, in aesthetics as in every other domain, the philosophy of Rūmī is inspired by the monistic idea. "The *Mathnawī*,"

[1] [This sentence has been added to the author's draft.—A. J. A.]

he says, "is the shop for Unity (*waḥdat*); anything that you see there except the One (God) is an idol." Ranging over the battlefield of existence, he finds all its conflicts and discords playing the parts assigned to them in the universal harmony which only mystics can realize.

Ṣūfī pantheism or monism involves the following propositions:

(*a*) There is One Real Being, the Ultimate Ground of all existence. This Reality may be viewed either as God (the Divine Essence) or as the World (phenomena by which the hidden Essence is made manifest).

(*b*) There is no creation in Time. Divine Self-manifestation is a perpetual process. While the *forms* of the universe change and pass and are simultaneously renewed without a moment's intermission, in its *essence* it is co-eternal with God. There never was a time when it did not exist as a whole in His Knowledge.

(*c*) God is both Immanent, in the sense that He appears under the aspect of limitation in all phenomenal forms, and Transcendent, in the sense that He is the Absolute Reality above and beyond every appearance.

(*d*) The Divine Essence is unknowable. God makes His Nature known to us by Names and Attributes which He has revealed in the Koran. Though essentially identical, from our point of view the Divine Attributes are diverse and opposed to each other, and this differentiation constitutes the phenomenal world, without which we could not distinguish good from evil and come to know the Absolute Good. In the sphere of Reality there is no such thing as evil.

(*e*) According to the Holy Tradition, "I created the creatures in order than I might be known," the entire content of God's Knowledge is objectified in the universe and pre-eminently in Man. The Divine Mind, which rules and animates the cosmos as an Indwelling Rational Principle (Logos), displays itself completely in the Perfect Man. The supreme type of the Perfect Man is the pre-existent Reality or Spirit of Muḥammad, whose "Light" irradiates the long series of prophets beginning with Adam and, after them, the hierarchy of Muslim saints, who are Muḥammad's spiritual heirs. Whether prophet or saint, the Perfect Man has realized his Oneness with God: he is the authentic image and manifestation of God and therefore the final cause of creation, since only through him does God become fully conscious of Himself.

These are some of the themes underlying Rūmī's poetry. He is not their original author; they may be regarded as having been gradually evolved by the long succession of Ṣūfī thinkers from the ninth century onwards, then gathered together and finally formulated by the famous Andalusian mystic, Ibnu'l-'Arabī (1165–1240). Ibnu'l-'Arabī has every right to be called the father of Islamic pantheism. He devoted colossal powers of intellect and imagination to constructing a system which, though it lacks order and connexion, covers the whole ground in detail and perhaps, all things considered, is the most imposing monument of mystical speculation the world has ever seen. While it is evident that Rūmī borrowed some part of his terminology and ideas from his elder contemporary, who himself travelled in Rum and lies buried in Damascus, the amount of the debt has inevitably been exaggerated by later commentators whose minds are filled with forms of thought alien to the *Mathnawi* but familiar to readers of Ibnu'l-'Arabī's *Fuṣūṣu'l-ḥikam* ("Bezels of Wisdom") and *al-Futūḥātu'l-Makkiyya* ("Meccan Revelations"). The Andalusian always writes with a fixed *philosophical* purpose, which may be defined as the *logical* development of a single all-embracing concept, and much of his thought expresses itself in a dialectic bristling with technicalities. Rūmī has no such aim. As E. H. Whinfield said, his mysticism is not "doctrinal" in the Catholic sense but "experimental." He appeals to the heart more than to the head, scorns the logic of the schools, and nowhere does he embody in philosophical

24

language even the elements of a system. The words used by Dante in reference to the *Divine Commedia* would serve excellently as a description of the *Mathnawī*: "the poem belongs to the moral or ethical branch of philosophy, its quality is not speculative but practical, and its ultimate end is to lead into the state of felicity those now enduring the miserable life of man." The *Mathnawī* for the most part shows Rūmī as the perfect spiritual guide engaged in making others perfect and furnishing novice and adept alike with matter suitable to their needs. Assuming the general monistic theory to be well known to his readers, he gives them a panoramic view of the Ṣūfī gnosis (direct intuition of God) and kindles their enthusiasm by depicting the rapture of those who "break through to the Oneness" and see all mysteries revealed.[1]

While the *Mathnawī* is generally instructional in character, though it also has entertaining passages, as befits a book intended for the enlightenment of all sorts of disciples, the *Diwān* and, on a much smaller scale, the *Rubāʿiyāt* are personal and emotional in appeal. Lyrics and quatrains alike have everywhere the authentic ring of spiritual inspiration, while in image, style and language they often approximate very closely to the *Mathnawī*. In some of these poems the mystic's passion is so exuberant, his imagination so overflowing, that we catch glimpses of the very madness of Divine experience. Yet the powerful intellect of Rūmī the man never quite capitulates to the enthusiasm of Rūmī the mystic; at the last moment there is a sudden drawing-back, a consciousness that certain matters are too secret and too holy to be communicated in words. It is not surprising to read that these poems, chanted (as many of them were doubtless composed) in the spiritual séance of the Mevlevis, roused the hearers to an almost uncontrollable fervour.

In Rūmī the Persian mystical genius found its supreme expression. Viewing the vast landscape of Ṣūfī poetry, we

[1] Here Professor Nicholson's notes end.

see him standing out as a sublime mountain-peak; the many other poets before and after him are but foot-hills in comparison. The influence of his example, his thought and his language is powerfully felt through all the succeeding centuries; every Ṣūfī after him capable of reading Persian has acknowledged his unchallenged leadership. To the West, now slowly realizing the magnitude of his genius, thanks in greatest measure to the work of that fine scholar whose last writings are contained in these pages, he is fully able to prove a source of inspiration and delight not surpassed by any other poet in the world's literature.

APPENDIX

NOTE

Most interesting of the biographical materials on Rūmī is the *Ibtidā-nāmah* ("Book of Beginning") a long narrative poem composed by Rūmī's son Sulṭān Walad; valuable information is also contained in the *Manāqibu'l-'ārifīn* ("Virtues of the Gnostics") of Aflākī, disciple of the poet's grandson Chelebī 'Ārif, which C. Huart translated as *Les Saints des derviches tourneurs* (Paris, 1918–22). In addition we have a number of books, like the *Fīhi mā fīhi* ("In it what is In it") (published at Teheran and Azamgarh in 1928) and the *Maqālāt-i Shams-i Tabrīz* ("Discourses of Shams-i Tabrīz") (still unedited), which, though shedding little light upon the life, go far to illuminate the ideas and doctrines of the poet.

In modern times the Persian scholar Badī'u'l-Zamān Furūzānfarr has written a valuable critical study of Rūmī's life [*Sharḥ-i ḥāl-i Maulānā* ("Biography of our Master"), Teheran 1932], and the learned Dr. H. Ritter has contributed a bio-bibliographical review of the whole subject (in *Der Islam*, 1940, 1942) which is as masterly as it is indispensable to any interested in this field of research.

PRELUDE[1]

⌣͡⌣͡⌣͡⌣͡⌣͡⌣͡⌣͡⌣͡⌣͡⌣͡

DEEP in our hearts the Light of Heaven is shining
    Upon a soundless Sea without a shore.
Oh, happy they who found it in resigning
    The images of all that men adore.

Blind eyes, to dote on shadows of things fair
    Only at last to curse their fatal lure,
Like Harut and Marut, that Angel-pair
    Who deemed themselves the purest of the pure.

Our ignorance and self-will and vicious pride
    Destroy the harmony of part and whole.
In vain we seek with lusts unmortified
    A vision of the One Eternal Soul.

Love, Love alone can kill what seemed so dead,
    The frozen snake[2] of passion. Love alone,
By tearful prayer and fiery longing fed,
    Reveals a knowledge schools have never known.

---

[1] This is not a translation—it has no original text behind it. I wrote to please myself, but seeing that it brings together some of Rūmī's characteristic ideas in a simple and compendious form, I think it may well serve as an overture to the present work.

[2] The "frozen snake," or dragon, which symbolizes the carnal soul, is never so dangerous as when it pretends to have been utterly subdued and crushed. In the *Mathnawī* Rūmī relates how a hunter discovered this monstrous creature half buried in snow. To all appearance it had been killed by the intense frost. He conveyed it to Baghdad, opened a public show, and announced that on payment of a small fee it might be viewed by any one whose curiosity it excited. Spectators came in crowds, but now the season had changed. Reviving under the fierce heat of a Mesopotamian summer, the dragon began to uncoil. The ensuing havoc and slaughter were terrible to see.

29

God's lovers learn from Him the secret ways
  Of Providence, the universal plan.
Living in Him, they ever sing His praise
  Who made the myriad worlds of Time for Man.

Evil they knew not, for in Him there's none;
  Yet without evil how should good be seen?
Love answers: "Feel with me, with me be one;
  Where I am, naught stands up to come between."

There are degrees of Heavenly Light in souls:
  Prophets and Saints have shown the Path they
      trod,
Its starting points and stages, halts and goals,
  All leading to the single end in God.

Love will not let his faithful servants tire,
  Immortal Beauty draws them on and on
From glory unto glory, drawing nigher
  At each remove and loving to be drawn.

When Truth shines out words fail and nothing tell;
Now hear the Voice within your hearts. Farewell.

I

THE SONG OF THE REED[1]

HEARKEN to this Reed forlorn,
Breathing, even since 'twas torn
From its rushy bed, a strain
Of impassioned love and pain.

"The secret of my song, though near,
None can see and none can hear.
Oh, for a friend to know the sign[2]
And mingle all his soul with mine!

'Tis the flame of Love that fired me,
'Tis the wine of Love inspired me.
Wouldst thou learn how lovers bleed,
Hearken, hearken to the Reed!"

---

[1] *Math.* I, 1. The opening lines of the poem strike a keynote that recurs insistently throughout. The Persian reed-flute (*nay*) has always been associated with the religious services of the Maulawī Order, in which music and dancing are prominent features. Rūmī uses it as a symbol for the soul emptied of self and filled with the Divine spirit. This blessed soul, during its life on earth, remembers the union with God which it enjoyed in eternity and longs ardently for deliverance from the world where it is a stranger and exile.

[2] *i.e.* a soul of its own kind. Only the mystic understands the mystic.

31

II

⌣⌣⌣⌣⌣⌣⌣⌣⌣⌣⌣

REMEMBERED MUSIC[1]

'Tɪs said, the pipe and lute that charm our
    ears
Derive their melody from rolling spheres;[2]
But Faith, o'erpassing speculation's bound,
Can see what sweetens every jangled sound.[3]

We, who are parts of Adam, heard with him
The song of angels and of seraphim.
Our memory, though dull and sad, retains
Some echo still of those unearthly strains.

Oh, music is the meat of all who love,
Music uplifts the soul to realms above.
The ashes glow, the latent fires increase:
We listen and are fed with joy and peace.

---

[1] *Math.* IV, 733.
[2] The well-known theory of Pythagoras is almost a commonplace in
Moslem philosophy and poetry. According to the Pure Brethren (*Ikh-
wānu 'l-ṣafā*) of Basra, "since the celestial spheres revolve and the planets
and stars are moved, it follows that they must have musical notes and
expressions with which God is glorified, delighting the souls of the
angels, just as in the corporeal world our souls listen with delight to
melodies and obtain relief from care and sorrow. And inasmuch as these
melodies are but echoes of heavenly music, they recall to us the spacious
gardens of Paradise and the pleasures enjoyed by the souls dwelling
there; and then our souls long to fly up thither and rejoin their mates."
[3] Ṣūfīs associate the spiritual influence of music with the pre-existence
of the soul. While listening, they hear again the Voice of God to which
all human souls responded in eternity (*Qur'ān* VII, 171) and the
anthems of the Heavenly Host.

III

LOVE IN ABSENCE[1]

How should not I mourn, like night, without His day and
the favour of His day-illuming countenance?

His unsweetness is sweet to my soul: may my soul be
sacrificed to the Beloved who grieves my heart!

I am in love with grief and pain for the sake of pleasing
my peerless King.

Tears shed for His sake are pearls, though people think
they are tears.

I complain of the Soul of my soul, but in truth I am not
complaining: I am only telling.[2]

My heart says it is tormented by Him, and I have long
been laughing at its poor pretence.[3]

Do me right, O Glory of the righteous, O Thou Who art
the dais, and I the threshold of Thy door!

Where are threshold and dais in reality? Where the
Beloved is, where are "we" and "I"?

O Thou Whose soul is free from "we" and "I", O Thou
Who art the essence of the spirit in men and women,

When men and women become one, Thou art that One;
when the units are wiped out, lo, Thou art that Unity.[4]

---

[1] *Math.* I, 1776.

[2] While self-conscious lovers complain of separation from the beloved
one and reproach her for her cruelty, the mystic's complaint (*shikāyat*)
is really no more than the tale (*ḥikāyat*) of his infinite longing for God—
a tale which God inspires him to tell.

[3] *i.e.* "I know that my anguish is a token of God's Loving-kindness."

[4] All phenomena are individualized modes of Real Being; when
stripped of their individuality, they become one with each other and
with Real Being. Hence God reveals Himself in every union of loving
souls.

Thou didst contrive this "I" and "we" in order to play
  the game of worship with Thyself,[5]
That all "I's" and "thou's" might become one soul and at
  last be submerged in the Beloved.

---

[5] Essentially God is both the Object of worship and the worshipper.
The illusion of individuality—"I" and "we"—arises from the interplay
of two opposite aspects, essence and form, under which the One Reality
may be regarded.

IV

⌐⌐⌐⌐⌐⌐⌐⌐⌐⌐⌐

"THE MARRIAGE OF TRUE MINDS"[1]

HAPPY the moment when we are seated in the palace, thou
and I,

With two forms and with two figures but with one soul,
thou and I.

The colours of the grove and the voices of the birds will
bestow immortality

At the time when we shall come into the garden, thou
and I.

The stars of Heaven will come to gaze upon us:

We shall show them the moon herself, thou and I.

Thou and I, individuals no more, shall be mingled in
ecstasy,

Joyful and secure from foolish babble, thou and I.

All the bright-plumed birds of Heaven will devour their
hearts with envy

In the place where we shall laugh in such a fashion, thou
and I.

This is the greatest wonder, that thou and I, sitting here
in the same nook,

Are at this moment both in 'Irāq and Khorāsān, thou
and I.

---

[1] *Dīwān, S. P.*, XXXVIII. A description of mystical union, in which
the antithesis of "lover" and "beloved" is resolved by their transmuta-
tion into the Universal Essence of Love.

V

"A SLEEP AND A FORGETTING"[1]

ONE who has lived many years in a city, so soon as he
goes to sleep,

Beholds another city full of good and evil, and his own
city vanishes from his mind.

He does not say to himself, "This is a new city: I am a
stranger here";

Nay, he thinks he has always lived in this city and was
born and bred in it.

What wonder, then, if the soul does not remember her
ancient abode and birth-place,

Since she is wrapt in the slumber of this world, like a star
covered by clouds?—

Especially as she has trodden so many cities and the dust
that darkens her vision is not yet swept away.[2]

---

[1] *Math.* IV, 3628.

[2] See No. CXVIII. The "cities" are the planes of being or phases of
experience traversed by the soul in its journeys *from* and *to* God, *i.e.* its
descent from the real to the phenomenal world and its subsequent
return from plurality to Unity.

VI

THE GRIEF OF THE DEAD[1]

THE Prince of mankind (Mohammed) said truly that no
one who has passed away from this world

Feels sorrow and regret for having died; nay, but he feels
a hundred regrets for having missed the opportunity,

Saying to himself, "Why did I not make death my object—
death which is the store-house of all fortunes and riches,[2]

And why, through seeing double, did I fasten my lifelong
gaze upon those phantoms that vanished at the fated
hour?"

The grief of the dead is not on account of death; it is
because they dwelt on the phenomenal forms of existence

And never perceived that all this foam is moved and fed
by the Sea.[3]

When the Sea has cast the foam-flakes on the shore, go to
the graveyard and behold them!

Say to them, "Where is your swirling onrush now?" and
hear them answer mutely, "Ask this question of the Sea,
not of us."

How should the foam fly without the wave? How should
the dust rise to the zenith without the wind?

Since you have seen the dust, see the Wind; since you have
seen the foam, see the Ocean of Creative Energy.

Come, see it, for insight is the only thing in you that avails:

---

[1] *Math.* VI, 1450. Cf. No. XXVII.
[2] Here "death" signifies "dying to self" (*fanā*). Cf. the Prophet's
saying, "Die before ye die."
[3] God is the only real Agent. All movement and life in the Universe
proceeds from Him.

the rest of you is a piece of fat and flesh, a woof and warp (of bones and sinews).

Dissolve your whole body into Vision: become seeing, seeing, seeing!

One sight discerns but a yard or two of the road; another surveys the temporal and spiritual worlds and beholds the Face of their King.

VII

⌐⌐⌐⌐⌐⌐⌐⌐⌐⌐⌐

THE UNREGENERATE[1]

IF any one were to say to the embryo in the womb, "Outside is a world well-ordered,

A pleasant earth, broad and long, wherein are a thousand delights and many things to eat;

Mountains and seas and plains, fragrant orchards, gardens and sown fields,

A sky very lofty and full of light, sunshine and moonbeams and innumerable stars;

Its wonders are beyond description: why dost thou stay, drinking blood, in this dungeon of filth and pain?"—

The embryo, being what it is, would turn away in utter disbelief; for the blind have no imagination.

So, in this world, when the saints tell of a world without scent and hue,

None of the vulgar hearkens to them: sensual desire is a barrier huge and stout—

Even as the embryo's craving for the blood that nourishes it in its low abodes

Debarred it from the perception of the external world, since it knows no food but blood.

---

[1] *Math.* III, 53. The analogy of childbirth and weaning to spiritual regeneration is developed in many passages of the *Mathnawí*.

VIII

THE BURDEN OF EXISTENCE[1]

FROM Thee first came this ebb and flow from within me;
else, O Glorious One, my sea was still.

Now, from the same source whence Thou broughtest this
trouble on me, graciously send me comfort!

O Thou Whose affliction makes men weak as women, show
me the one path, do not let me follow ten!

I am like a jaded camel: the saddle of free-will has sorely
bruised my back

With its heavy panniers sagging from this side to that
in turn.

Let the ill-balanced load drop from me, so that I may
browse in the Meadow of Thy Bounty.

Hundreds of thousands of years I was flying to and fro
involuntarily, like a mote in the air.

If I have forgotten that time and state, yet the migration
in sleep recalls it to my memory.

At night I escape from this four-branched cross into the
spacious pastures of the spirit.[2]

From the nurse, Sleep, I suck the milk of those bygone
days of mine, O Lord.

All mortals are fleeing from their free-will and self-existence
to their unconscious selves.

They lay upon themselves the opprobrium of wine and
minstrelsy in order that for awhile they may be delivered
from self-consciousness.

All know that this existence is a snare, that will and thought
and memory are a hell.

---

[1] *Math.* VI, 210.
[2] See No. XIII. "This four-branched cross" alludes to the four elements
which compose the prison-house where the fallen soul is crucified.

IX

THE SPIRIT OF THE SAINTS[1]

THERE is a Water that flows down from Heaven
To cleanse the world of sin by grace Divine.
At last, its whole stock spent, its virtue gone,
Dark with pollution not its own, it speeds
Back to the Fountain of all purities;
Whence, freshly bathed, earthward it sweeps again,
Trailing a robe of glory bright and pure.

This Water is the Spirit of the Saints,
Which ever sheds, until itself is beggared,
God's balm on the sick soul; and then returns
To Him who made the purest light of Heaven.

---

[1] *Math.* V, 200. Through absorption (*istighrāq*) in the Creator of spiritual energy the saints are revived and strengthened for their task "of pure ablution round earth's human shores."

X

THE CHILDREN OF LIGHT[1]

BEYOND the stars are Stars in which there is no combust
    nor sinister aspect,[2]

Stars moving in other Heavens, not the seven heavens
    known to all,

Stars immanent in the radiance of the Light of God,
    neither joined to each other nor separate.[3]

Whoso hath his fortune from these Stars, his soul drives
    off and consumes the unbelievers.[4]

God sprinkled His Light over all spirits, but only the blest
    held up their skirts to receive it;

And, having gained that largesse of light, they turned their
    faces away from all but God.[5]

That which is of the sea is going to the sea: it is going to
    the place whence it came—

From the mountain the swift-rushing torrent, and from our
    body the soul whose motion is inspired by love.[6]

---

[1] *Math.* I, 754.

[2] "Combust" (*iḥtirāq*), an astronomical term for the conjunction of
one of the five planets (Venus, Mercury, Mars, Jupiter and Saturn)
with the sun in the same degree of the Zodiac.

[3] While dispositions in the physical world are said to be influenced
by the planets, the fortune of the elect comes from spiritual luminaries
shining eternally in the heaven of the Divine Essence. These "Stars"
are the Names and Attributes of God which determine every phase of
the mystic's life. In so far as they are diverse in their effects they are not
inseparable; but from a higher point of view they inhere in the Un-
differentiated Essence and are identical with It and with each other.

[4] The radiant souls of the elect consume infidelity in the same way
as shooting stars burn the devils pelted with them (*Qur'ān* LXVII, 5).

[5] According to the *Ḥadīth*: "God created the creatures in darkness,
then He sprinkled some of His Light upon them. Those whom it reached
took the right path, while those whom it missed went astray."

[6] Every "part" seeks its "whole": the "Fünkelein der Seele" is
impelled by love towards the Universal Light whence it sprang.

XI

⌣⌐⌣⌐⌣⌐⌣⌐⌣⌐⌣⌐⌣⌐⌣⌐⌣⌐⌣

LOVE, THE HIEROPHANT[1]

'Tis heart-ache lays the lover's passion bare:
No sickness with heart-sickness may compare.
Love is a malady apart, the sign
And astrolabe of mysteries Divine.[2]
Whether of heavenly mould or earthly cast,
Love still doth lead us Yonder at the last.[3]
Reason, explaining Love, can naught but flounder
Like ass in mire: Love is Love's own expounder.
Does not the sun himself the sun declare?[4]
Behold him! All the proof thou seek'st is there.

---

[1] *Math.* I, 109.

[2] "Man is God's astrolabe, and just as by means of an astrolabe the astronomer discovers the conditions of the celestial spheres and observes the motions and influences of the stars, so when Man has received from God the gift of self-knowledge, he continually beholds the manifestation of the Divine Beauty, which is without attributes and beyond description, by means of the astrolabe of his existence, which is a Divine mirror wherein that Beauty never ceases to be displayed." (*Fīhi mā fīhi*, 13).

[3] So Emerson: "Beholding in many souls the traits of the divine beauty, and separating in each soul that which is divine from the taint which it has contracted in the world, the lover ascends to the highest beauty, to the love and knowledge of the Divinity by steps on this ladder of created souls."

[4] *Āftāb āmad dalīl-i āftāb*, a famous and oft-repeated analogy.

XII

THE LOVE OF WOMAN[1]

If you rule your wife outwardly, yet inwardly you are
ruled by her whom you desire,

This is characteristic of Man: in other animals love is
lacking, and that shows their inferiority.[2]

The Prophet said that woman prevails over the wise, while
ignorant men prevail over her; for in them the fierceness
of the animal is immanent.

Love and tenderness are human qualities, anger and lust
are animal qualities.

Woman is a ray of God: she is not the earthly beloved.
She is creative: you might say she is not created.[3]

---

[1] *Math.* I, 2431.

[2] Although animals relatively to Man are deficient in love, they
"know what love is" and "he that is blind to love is inferior to a dog"
(*Math.* V, 2008).

[3] Sweeping aside the veil of form, the poet beholds in woman the
eternal Beauty, the inspirer and object of all love, and regards her, in
her essential nature, as the medium through which that Beauty reveals
itself and exercises creative activity. Ibnu'l-'Arabī went so far as to say
that the most perfect vision of God is enjoyed by those who contemplate
Him in woman.

XIII

DIVINE BEAUTY[1]

KINGS lick the earth whereof the fair are made,
For God hath mingled in the dusty earth
A draught of Beauty from His choicest cup.
'Tis *that*, fond lover—not these lips of clay—
Thou art kissing with a hundred ecstasies,
Think, then, what must it be when undefiled!

------

[1] *Math.* V, 372.

XIV

"I TURN TOWARD THEE"[1]

O THOU Who art my soul's comfort in the season of sorrow,
O Thou Who art my spirit's treasure in the bitterness of
    death!
That which the imagination hath not conceived, that
    which the understanding hath not seen,
Visiteth my soul from Thee; hence in worship I turn
    toward Thee.
By Thy Grace I keep fixed on eternity my amorous gaze,
Except, O King, the pomps that perish lead me astray.
The favour of him who brings glad tidings of Thee,
Even without Thy summons, is sweeter in mine ear than
    songs.
If the never-ceasing Bounty should offer kingdoms,
If the Hidden Treasure should set before me all that is,
I would bow down with my soul, I would lay my face in
    the dust,
I would cry, "Of all these the love of such an One for me!"

---

[1] *Dīwān, SP,* VI.

XV

⌣⌣⌣⌣⌣⌣⌣⌣⌣⌣

THE TRUTH WITHIN US[1]

'Twas a fair orchard, full of trees and fruit
And vines and greenery. A Ṣūfī there
Sat with eyes closed, his head upon his knee,
Sunk deep in meditation mystical.
"Why," asked another, "dost thou not behold
These Signs of God the Merciful displayed
Around thee, which He bids us contemplate?"
"The signs," he answered, "I behold within;
Without is naught but symbols of the Signs."

What is all beauty in the world? The image,
Like quivering boughs reflected in a stream,
Of that eternal Orchard which abides
Unwithered in the hearts of Perfect Men.

---

[1] *Math.* IV, 1358. An early parallel occurs in the legend of Rābi'ah al-'Adawiyyah. One day in spring-time she entered her house and bowed her head. "Come out," said the woman-servant, "and behold what God hath made." Rābi'ah answered, "Come in and behold the Maker."

XVI

MYSTICS KNOW[1]

SINCE Wisdom is the true believer's stray camel,[2] he
knows it with certainty, from whomsoever he may have
heard of it,

And when he finds himself face to face with it, how should
there be doubt? How can he mistake?

If you tell a thirsty man—"Here is a cup of water: drink!"—

Will he reply?—"This is mere assertion: let me alone, O
liar, go away."

Or suppose a mother cries to her babe, "Come, I am mother:
hark my child!"—

Will it say?—"Prove this to me, so that I may take comfort
in thy milk."

When in the heart of a people there is spiritual perception,
the face and voice of the prophet are as an evidentiary
miracle.

When the prophet utters a cry from without, the soul of
the people falls to worship within,

Because never in the world will the soul's ear have heard
a cry of the same kind as his.

That wondrous voice is heard by the soul in exile—the voice
of God calling, "*Lo, I am nigh.*"[3]

---

[1] *Math.* II, 3591, a passage illustrating the Platonic doctrine of
anamnesis and the self-evidence of truth revealed in mystical
experience.

[2] A saying ascribed to 'Alī. The Faithful seek the knowledge of
God which they possessed in past eternity and recognize it immediately
when found.

[3] *Qur'ān* II, 182.

XVII

‿‿‿‿‿‿‿‿‿‿

ASLEEP TO THE WORLD[1]

Every night Thou dost free our spirits from the body's snare and erase all impressions on the tablets (of memory).

Our spirits are set free every night from this cage, they are done with audience and talk and tale.

At night prisoners forget their prison, at night governors forget their power.

There is no sorrow, no thought of gain or loss, no idea of this person or that person.

Such is the state of the mystic, even when he is not asleep: God saith, "(*Thou wouldst deem them awake*) *whilst they slept.*"[2]

He is asleep, day and night, to the affairs of this world, like a pen in the hand of the Lord.[3]

God hath shown forth some part of his state, inasmuch as the vulgar too are carried away by sleep:

Their spirits gone into the Wilderness that is beyond words, Their souls and bodies at rest.

Till with a whistle Thou callest them back to the snare, bringest them all again to justice and judgement.[4]

---

[1] *Math.* I, 388.

[2] An allusion to the legend of the Seven Sleepers of Ephesus related in *Qur'ān* XVIII, 8–25.

[3] Cf. the Tradition that "the true believer is between the two fingers of God the Merciful." According as God reveals Himself in the aspect of Majesty (wrath and terror) or Beauty (mercy and love) the mystic's heart contracts with grief or expands with joy.

[4] *i.e.* to their self-conscious life in the present world, which is a court of Divine justice where mankind are on trial.

At daybreak, like Isrāfīl (Seraphiel), He bids them return
   from Yonder to the world of form :5
The disembodied spirits He confines anew and causes each
   body to be laden (with its good and evil works).

----

5 This action of God resembles that of the Archangel Isrāfīl, whose
trumpet-blast at the Resurrection will give the signal for the spirits of
the dead to rejoin their bodies.

XVIII

THE FAITHFUL ARE ONE SOUL[1]

THE Faithful are many, but their Faith is one; their bodies
are numerous, but their soul is one.

Besides the understanding and soul which is in the ox and
the ass, Man has another intelligence and soul.

Again, in the owner of the Divine breath, there is a soul
other than the human soul.[2]

The animal soul does not possess oneness: do not seek
oneness from that airy spirit.

If its owner eat bread, his neighbour is not filled; if he bear
a load, his neighbour does not become laden;

Nay, but he rejoices at his neighbour's death and dies of
envy when he sees his neighbour prosperous.

The souls of wolves and dogs are separate; the souls of the
Lions of God are united.

I speak nominally of their souls in the plural, for that single
Soul is a hundred in relation to the body,

Just as the single light of the sun in heaven is a hundred in
relation to the house-courts on which it shines;

But when you remove the walls, all these scattered lights
are one and the same.

When the bodily houses have no foundation remaining, the
Faithful remain one soul.

---

[1] *Math.* IV, 408. When Rūmī speaks of "the Faithful," he generally
means inspired men, who alone have the real faith that springs from
immediate experience of the Divine.

[2] The three souls mentioned here are known in Ṣūfī psychology as
(*a*) the animal or sensual; (*b*) the intelligential (discursive reason); and
(*c*) the transcendental (Universal Reason), which displays itself in
prophets and saints.

XIX

THE LADDER TO HEAVEN[1]

THE worldly sense is the ladder to this world; the religious sense is the ladder to Heaven.

Seek the well-being of that sense from the physician; beg the well-being of this sense from the man beloved of God.[2]

The spiritual way ruins the body and, having ruined it, restores it to prosperity:

Ruined the house for the sake of the golden treasure, and with that same treasure builds it better than before;[3]

Cut off the water and cleansed the river-bed, then caused drinking-water to flow in it;[4]

Cleft the skin and drew out the barb, then made fresh skin grow over the wound;

Razed the fortress and took it from the infidel, then reared thereon a hundred towers and ramparts.[5]

Sometimes the action of God appears like this, sometimes the contrary: (true) religion is nothing but bewilderment.

---

[1] *Math.* I, 303.

[2] *i.e.* the saintly healer of souls.

[3] The spiritual essence of Man is buried in his earthly nature, as a treasure beneath the floor of a house.

[4] Purification of the heart cannot begin till the "water" of lust, passion, and all sensuous ideas has been cut off.

[5] Ghazālī likens the body to a fortress in which God has placed the spirit or rational soul with orders to defend it against the "infidel," *i.e.* the carnal soul. When it is occupied by evil passions, the spirit must destroy it, expel the invaders, and then rebuild it and make it impregnable.

(I mean) not one bewildered in such wise that his back is
  turned on Him; nay, but one bewildered and drowned
  and drunken with the Beloved.[6]
His face is set towards (devoted to) the Beloved, while the
  other's face is just his own.
Look long on the face of everyone, watch attentively: it
  may be that by doing service (to Ṣūfīs) you will come
  to know the face (of the Saint).
Since many a devil hath the face of Adam, you should not
  put a hand in every hand;
For as the fowler whistles to decoy a bird he is bent on
  catching,
Which hears the note of its mate and comes down from the
  air and finds itself entrapped,
So does a vile man steal the language of dervishes to fas-
  cinate and deceive one who is simple.
The work of holy men is as light and heat; the work of the
  ungodly is trickery and shamelessness.

---

[6] The discursive reason, contemplating apparently irreconcilable
forms of Divine action, is bewildered. But the bewilderment (ḥayrat) of
mystics dazzled by nearness to the Light of God must not be confused
with that of religious hypocrites who have lost their way in a maze of
ignorance and error.

XX

⌐⌐⌐⌐⌐⌐⌐⌐⌐⌐

THE TRUE ṢŪFĪ[1]

WHAT makes the Ṣūfī? Purity of heart;
Not the patched mantle and the lust perverse
Of those vile earth-bound men who steal his name.
He in all dregs discerns the essence pure:
In hardship ease, in tribulation joy.
The phantom sentries, who with batons drawn
Guard Beauty's palace-gate and curtained bower,
Give way before him, unafraid he passes,
And showing the King's arrow, enters in.[2]

---

[1]. *Math.* V, 358.
[2] An arrow inscribed with the king's name was handed to a sur-
rendering enemy in token that his safety was guaranteed. Saʿdī alludes
to this custom in the verse:

"Either thou wilt shoot a deadly arrow at my wounded heart
And take my life, or thou wilt give me the arrow of indemnity
(*tīr-i amān*)."

XXI

⎣⎯⎤⎣⎯⎤⎣⎯⎤⎣⎯⎤⎣⎯⎤⎣⎯⎤⎣⎯⎤⎣⎯⎤⎣⎯⎤⎣⎯⎤

NOTHING VENTURE NOTHING WIN[1]

WHEN you put a cargo on board a ship, you make that
venture on trust,

For you know not whether you will be drowned or come
safe to land.

If you say, "I will not embark till I am certain of my fate,"
then you will do no trade: the secret of these two des-
tinies is never disclosed.

The faint-hearted merchant neither gains nor loses; nay
he loses: one must take fire in order to get light.

Since all affairs turn upon hope, surely Faith is the best
object of hope, for thereby you win salvation.

---

[1] *Math.* III, 3083. Though God has decreed in eternity that some
souls are saved and others lost, He commands the prophets to preach
His Word to all alike (*Qur'ān* V, 71). Obey it and trust in Him. Even
worldly success cannot be achieved without running risks.

XXII

⌐⌐⌐⌐⌐⌐⌐⌐⌐⌐

THE MAN WHO LOOKED BACK ON
HIS WAY TO HELL[1]

THE guardian angels, who used to walk unseen before and
behind him, have now become visible like policemen.

They drag him along, prodding him with goads and crying,
"Begone, O dog, to thy kennel!"

He looks back towards the Holy Presence: his tears fall
like autumn rain. A mere hope—what has he but
that?

Then from God in the realm of Light comes the command—
"Say ye to him: 'O ne'er-do-well destitute of merit,

Thou hast seen the black scroll of thy misdeeds. What dost
thou expect? Why art thou tarrying in vain?' "

He answers: "Lord, Thou knowest I am a hundred hundred
times worse than Thou hast declared;

But beyond my exertion and action, beyond good and evil
and faith and infidelity,

Beyond living righteously or behaving disobediently—
I had a great hope of Thy Loving-kindness.

I turn again to that pure Grace, I am not regarding my
own works.

Thou gavest me my being as a robe of honour: I have
always relied on that munificence."

---

[1] *Math.* V, 1815. The passage to which these verses belong is founded
on the following tradition: "When God has finished judging mankind
on the Day of Resurrection, two men will remain and the order will be
given that both are for Hell. Then on the way thither one of them will
turn his face to God, and the Almighty will order him to be brought
back and will ask him why he turned round, and he will answer, 'I was
hoping Thou wouldst let me enter Paradise.' And then God will order
that he be taken to Paradise."

When he confesses his sins, God saith to the Angels, "Bring
   him back, for he never lost hope of Me.
Like one who recks of naught, I will deliver him and cancel
   all his trespasses.
I will kindle such a fire of Grace that the least spark thereof
   consumes all sin and necessity and free-will.
I will set fire to the tenement of Man and make its thorns
   a bower of roses."

XXIII

SPIRITUAL CHURNING[1]

THY truth is concealed in falsehood, like the taste of butter in buttermilk.

Thy falsehood is this perishable body; thy truth is the lordly spirit.

During many years the buttermilk remains in view, while the butter has vanished as though it were naught,

Till God send a Messenger, a chosen Servant, to shake the buttermilk in the churn—

To shake it with method and skill, and teach me that my true self was hidden.[2]

The buttermilk is old: keep it, do not let it go till you extract the butter from it.

Turn it deftly to and fro, that it may give up its secret.

The mortal body is a proof of the immortal spirit: the maundering of the drunken reveller proves the existence of the cupbearer.

---

[1] *Math.* IV, 3030.

[2] It is the mission of the Sūfī Pīr to develop and bring out the spiritual qualities latent in his disciple, just as an infant learns to speak by listening to its mother.

⌣‚⌣‚⌣‚⌣‚⌣‚⌣‚⌣‚⌣‚⌣‚⌣

XXIV

THE BLIND FOLLOWER:[1]

THE parrot looking in the mirror sees
Itself, but not its teacher hid behind,
And learns the speech of Man, the while it
  thinks
A bird of its own sort is talking to it.[2]

So the disciple full of egoism
Sees nothing in the Shaykh except himself.
The Universal Reason eloquent
Behind the mirror of the Shaykh's discourse—
The Spirit which is the mystery of Man—
He cannot see. Words mimicked, learned by
  rote,
'Tis all. A parrot he, no bosom-friend!

---

[1] *Math.* V, 1430.
[2] Parrots in the East are trained to talk by means of a mirror, behind
which is a curtain. Allegorically the "mirror" is the holy man, who
serves as a medium between the "parrot," *i.e.* the disciple, and God, the
invisible Speaker and Teacher.

XXV

THE BIRDS OF SOLOMON[1]

THE eloquence of courtly birds is a mere echo: where is
the speech of the birds of Solomon?[2]

How wilt thou know their cries, when thou hast never seen
Solomon for a single moment?

Far beyond East and West are spread the wings of the bird
whose note thrills them that hear it:

From the Footstool of God to the earth and from the earth
to the Divine Throne it moves in glory and majesty.

The bird that goes without this Solomon is a bat in love
with darkness.

Make thyself familiar with Solomon, O miscreant bat,
lest thou remain in darkness for ever.

Go but one ell in that direction, and like the ell thou wilt
become the standard of measurement.[3]

Even by hopping lamely and limply in that direction thou
wilt be freed from all lameness and limpness.

---

[1] *Math.* II, 3758. Solomon was taught the bird language (*Qur'ān*
XXVII, 16). Here he represents the Perfect Man, *i.e.* the Sūfī *murshid*.

[2] All artificial eloquence, such as court poets display in their
panegyrics, is meaningless in comparison with the mystic utterances of
those whom God has inspired.

[3] Cf. the saying of Kharraqānī, "I attained to God as soon as I set
foot on the first step of the ladder." The Perfect Man is the ideal of
creation and the criterion by which the true value of everything is to be
judged.

XXVI

⌐,⌐,⌐,⌐,⌐,⌐,⌐,⌐,⌐,⌐,⌐

THE CARNAL SOUL[1]

YOUR self (*nafs*) is the mother of all idols: the material
idol is a snake, but the spiritual idol is a dragon.

'Tis easy to break an idol, very easy; to regard the self as
easy to subdue is folly, folly.

O son, if you would know the form of the self, read the
description of Hell with its seven gates.[2]

From the self at every moment issues an act of deceit; and
in each of those deceits a hundred Pharaohs and their
hosts are drowned.

---

[1] *Math.* I, 772.
[2] The *nafs* is Hell or a part of Hell; in essence it is one with the
Devil. Therefore Hell, being the nature of the *nafs-i ammārah* (the soul
that commands us to sin), is really subjective. The seven gates or limbos
of Hell typify the vices which lead to perdition (*muhlikāt*).

XXVII

THE BEAUTY OF DEATH[1]

HE who deems death to be lovely as Joseph gives up his
soul in ransom for it; he who deems it to be like the wolf
turns back from the path of salvation.

Every one's death is of the same quality as himself, my lad:
to the enemy of God an enemy, to the friend of God a
friend.[2]

In the eyes of the Turcoman the mirror is fair; in the eyes
of the Ethiopian it is dark as an Ethiopian.

Your fear of death is really fear of yourself: see what it is
from which you are fleeing!

'Tis your own ugly face, not the visage of Death: your
spirit is like the tree, and death like the leaf.

It has grown from you, whether it be good or evil: all your
hidden thoughts, foul or fair, are born from yourself.

If you are wounded by thorns, you planted them; and if
you are clad in satin and silk, *you* were the spinner.

Know that the act is not of the same complexion as its
result; a service rendered is not homogeneous with the
fragment given in return.

The labourer's wage is dissimilar to his work: the latter is
the accident, while the former is the substance.[3]

---

[1] *Math.* III, 3438. Cf. No. VI. The comparison with Joseph and the
wolf alludes to *Qur'ān* XII, 13 *seqq.*

[2] Death, whether physical (*iḍṭirārī*) or mystical (*ikhtiyārī*), is like a
mirror in which every one sees the image of himself: if his nature be
good and his actions righteous, he will be in love with death; otherwise
he will loathe it and flee in terror from the reflection of his own wickedness. What he dreads so much is really something conceived and produced by himself.

[3] Human action is both a cause and an effect. Man, in so far as he
acts freely, incurs retribution hereafter; but this, though from one
point of view a direct consequence of the action with which it corre-

The latter is wholly toil and effort and sweat, the former is
wholly silver and gold and viands.
When the worshipper has sown a prostration or genuflexion
here, it becomes the Garden of the Blest hereafter.
When praise of God has flown from his mouth, the Lord of
the Daybreak fashions it into a fruit of Paradise.

---

sponds in quality, may also be regarded as the final cause and eternal
form of the action, pre-existent in God's Knowledge, like the idea of a
house in the mind of the architect. Viewed in this way, retribution is a
Divine manifestation of the idea immanent in all that appears under
the form of human action or, in other words, a transformation of the
appearance with its underlying reality. Hence there can be no true
similarity between them: they differ as accident and substance. See
further, *Math.* II, 938—1000 with the commentary *ad loc.*

XXVIII

A PRAYER FOR GOOD BEHAVIOUR[1]

LET us beseech God to help us to self-control (*adab*): he
who lacks self-control is deprived of the grace of the
Lord.[2]

The undisciplined man does not corrupt himself alone: he
sets the whole world afire.

Whatever befalls thee of gloom and sorrow is the result of
thy irreverence and insolence.

Any one behaving with irreverence in the path of the
Friend is a brigand who robs men: he is no man.[3]

Through discipline Heaven was filled with light, through
discipline the Angels became immaculate and holy.[4]

By reason of irreverence the sun is eclipsed, and insolence
caused 'Azāzīl to be turned back from the door.[5]

---

[1] *Math.* I, 78.

[2] *Adab* may be defined as the character, feelings, and manners which
are the fruit of self-discipline and spiritual culture; like St. Paul's ἀγάπη
"it doth not behave itself unseemly."

[3] He has not mastered his passions and therefore does not deserve
the name of "man."

[4] Cf. Wordsworth's lines in the *Ode to Duty*:

"Thou dost preserve the Stars from wrong,
    And the most ancient Heavens, through thee, are fresh
    and strong."

[5] Eclipse is a Divine chastisement inflicted on the sun whenever it
presumed to deviate from its appointed course. 'Azāzīl was the name of
Iblīs before his fall.

XXIX

COMMUNION WITH THE SAINTS[1]

God rebuked Moses, saying. "O thou who hast seen the rising of the moon from thy bosom,[2]

Thou whom I have illumined with My Light! I am God, I fell sick, thou camest not."[3]

Moses said, "O transcendent One, Thou art clear of defect. What mystery is this? Explain, O Lord!"

God said unto him again, "Wherefore didst not thou kindly ask after Me when I was sick?"

He answered. "O Lord, Thou never ailest. My understanding is lost: unfold the meaning of these words."

God said. "Yea; a favourite and chosen slave of Mine fell sick. I am he. Consider well:

His infirmity is My infirmity, his sickness is My sickness."

Who ever would sit with God, let him sit in the presence of the Saints.

If you are separated from the presence of the Saints, you are in perdition, because you are a part without its whole.

Whomsoever the Devil cuts off from that noble company, he finds him with none to aid and devours him.

---

[1] *Math.* II, 2156.

[2] Mystic illumination is often likened to the White Hand of Moses. See *Qur'ān* VII, 105 and Exodus IV, 6.

[3] This passage on the oneness of God with His friends (*awliyā*) gives the gist of a Holy Tradition (*Ḥadīth-i qudsī*), beginning: "On the Day of Resurrection God most High will say, 'O Son of Adam, I was sick and thou didst not visit Me.'" Cf. St. Matthew, XXV, 43-45.

XXX

THE MAN WHO FLED FROM AZRAEL[1]

At morn, to Solomon in his hall of justice
A noble suitor came, running in haste,
His countenance pale with anguish, his lips blue.
"What ails, thee, Khwājah?" asked the King.
    Then he:
"'Twas Azrael—ah, such a look he cast
On me of rage and vengeance." "Come now, ask
What boon thou wilt." "Protector of our lives,
I pray thee, bid the Wind convey me straight
To Hindustān: thy servant, there arrived,
Shall peradventure save his soul from Death."

How folk do ever flee from dervishhood
Into the jaws of greed and idle hope!
Your fear of dervishhood is that doomed man's
    terror,
Greed and ambition are your Hindustān.[2]
Solomon bade the Wind transport him swiftly
Over the sea to farthest Hindustān.
On the morrow, when the King in audience sate,
He said to Azrael, "Wherefore didst thou look
Upon that Musulmān so wrathfully
His home knew him no more?" "Nay, not in
    wrath,"

---

[1] *Math.* I, 956
[2] "Dervishhood" is spiritual poverty, which means "dying to self," *i.e.* abandoning every "god" or object of desire except Allah. To shrink from this "death" and seek satisfaction in the pursuit of worldly goods is as vain and useless as to flee from Azrael.

Replied the Angel, "did I look on him;
But seeing him pass by, I stared in wonder,
For God had bidden me take his soul that day
In Hindustān. I stood there marvelling.
Methought, even if he had a hundred wings,
'Twere far for him to fly to Hindustān."

Judge all things of the world by this same rule
And ope your eyes and see! Away from whom
Shall we fly headlong? From ourselves?
   Absurd!
From God, then? Oh, the vain and woeful
   crime![3]

---

[3] It is absurd to suppose that we can escape from being what God
has predetermined and created us to be. Our freedom consists in not
being slaves to our passions or to anything whatsoever but God alone.

XXXI

"OMNES EODEM COGIMUR":[1]

EVERY blind wayfarer, be he righteous or wicked, God is
dragging, bound in chains, into His Presence.

All are dragged along this Way reluctantly, save those who
are acquainted with the mysteries of Divine action.

The command *Come against your will* is addressed to the
blind follower; *Come willingly* is for the man moulded of
truth.[2]

While the former, like an infant, loves the Nurse for the
sake of milk, the other has given his heart away to this
Veiled One.

The "infant" hath no knowledge of Her beauty: he wants
nothing of Her except milk;

The real lover of the Nurse is disinterested, single-minded
in pure devotion.

Whether God's seeker love Him for something other than
He, that he may continually partake of His good,

Or whether he love God for His Very Self, for naught
besides Him, lest he be separated from Him,

In either case the quest and aspiration proceed from that
Source: the heart is made captive by that Heart-ravisher.

---

[1] *Math.* III, 4581.
[2] See *Qur'ān* XLI, 10 and No. XCII *infra*.

XXXII

FAITH AND WORKS[1]

GOD hath placed a ladder before us: we must climb it,
  step by step.

You have feet: why pretend to be lame? You have hands:
  why conceal the fingers that grip?

Freewill is the endeavour to thank God for His Beneficence;
  your necessitarianism denies that Beneficence.

Thanksgiving for the power of acting freely gives you more
  power to thank Him; necessitarianism takes away what
  God hath given.

The brigands are on the road: do not sleep until you see
  the gate and the threshold![2]

If you put trust in God, trust Him with your work! Sow
  the seed, then rely upon the Almighty![3]

---

[1] *Math.* I, 929. The arguments for and against quietism (*tawakkul*,
trust in God) are set forth in the form of a dialogue between a lion and
the smaller animals on which he preys (*Math.* I, 900–991). *Tawakkul*,
no doubt, is fundamental; but does it imply that we should refrain from
using to the best of our ability the faculties of mind and body which
God has bestowed on us in order that we may attain to real Knowledge
of Him? On the contrary, to neglect these means (*asbāb*) is rank impiety
and ingratitude. Our throwing ourselves earnestly into the spiritual
warfare (*al-jihād al-akbar*), far from being a vain attempt to interfere
with the course of Providence, is a Divinely ordained duty, which all
prophets and saints have practised as well as preached.

[2] The "traveller" (*sālik*) on the Way to God must never rest. Only
when the goal is gained can he afford to "sleep," *i.e.* enjoy the mystical
state of quiet.

[3] Cf. the Prophet's advice to one who asked whether he should leave
his camel to God's care: "Tether her, then trust in Him."

XXXIII

"NO MONKERY IN ISLAM"[1]

"O PEACOCK, do not tear out thy feathers, but wean thy
heart from pride in them: the existence of a foe is indispensable for waging the Holy War.

There cannot be self-restraint in the absence of desire:
when there is no adversary, what avails thy courage?

Hark, do not castrate thyself, do not become a monk:
chastity depends on the existence of lust.

The Divine command '*Eat ye*' is the lure for appetite; then
comes '*Do not exceed*': that is temperance.[2]

Without the pain of self-denial there is no protasis; hence
the apodosis does not follow.[3]

How admirable is that protasis and how delightful is that
apodosis—a recompense enchanting the heart and
increasing the life of the spirit!"

---

[1] *Math.* V, 574. This apocryphal Ḥadīth, based on a questionable
interpretation of a passage in the *Qur'ān* (LVII, 27), is aimed at asceticism as practised by Christian hermits; and here Rūmī contrasts the
Ṣūfī Path of self-discipline and self-conquest with a method which, in
cutting off all temptations, deprives itself of the means whereby virtue
is tested and wisdom made perfect.

[2] See *Qur'ān* VII, 29.

[3] A grammatical analogy. The Ṣūfī's reward from God depends on
his self-denial in the same way as the consequence stated in the principal
clause of a conditional sentence depends on fulfilment of the condition
stated in the subordinate clause.

XXXIV

DO NOT TRAVEL ALONE[1]

I n our religion the approved thing is war and danger; in
the religion of Jesus it is flight to cave and mountain.[2]

The Sunnah is the safest road, and the community of the
Faithful your best fellow-travellers.

The Way to God is full of trouble and bale: it is not the
way for any one whose nature is effeminate.

On this road men's souls are tried by terror, as a sieve is
used for sifting bran.

If you go by yourself, I grant that you may manage to
escape the wolf; but you will feel no spiritual alacrity.

The ass, notwithstanding its grossness, is encouraged and
strengthened, O dervish, by comrades of its own kind.

How many more goadings and cudgellings does it suffer
when it crosses the desert without company!

It says to you implicitly, "Take good heed! Don't travel
alone unless you are an ass!"

---

[1] *Math.* VI, 494.

[2] Rūmī adopts the traditional Moslem view of "the religion of
Jesus," a view derived from early Moslem ascetics who took the solitary
rāhib as their model, while Ṣūfīs, with few exceptions, have not only
embraced but developed the idea of brotherhood so characteristic of
religious life in Islam.

XXXV

FINE FEATHERS[1]

"Needs must I tear them out," the peacock
   cried,
"These gorgeous plumes which only tempt my
   pride."

Of all his talents let the fool beware:
Mad for the bait, he never sees the snare.
Harness to fear of God thy strength and skill,
Else there's no bane so deadly as free-will.

---

[1] *Math.* V, 648. Human powers and capacities, unless devoted to the
service of God, breed false confidence and bring disaster. The moral,
however, is not that we must deliberately throw away the weapons
without which the victory over ourselves cannot be won, but that we
should beware of relying on them and taking credit for any success they
enable us to achieve.

XXXVI

THE TREASURE-SEEKER[1]

HE was engaged in this prayer when a Voice came from
Heaven, saying,

"You were told to put the arrow to the bow; but who told
you to shoot with all your might?

Self-conceit caused you to raise the bow aloft and display
your skill in archery.

You must put the arrow to the bow, but do not draw to
the full extent of your power.

Where the arrow falls, dig and search! Trust not in
strength, seek the treasure by means of piteous
supplication."

That which is real is nearer than the neck-artery, and you
have shot the arrow of thought far afield.[2]

The philosopher kills himself with thinking. Let him run
on: his back is turned to the treasure.

Most of those destined for Paradise are simpletons, so that
they escape from the mischief of philosophy.[3]

While the clever ones are pleased with the device, the
simple ones rest, like babes, in the bosom of the Deviser.

---

[1] *Math.* VI, 2347. A dervish dreamed that a Voice from Heaven bade
him go to the shop of a certain stationer, where he would find a scroll
containing the clue to a hidden treasure. On awaking, he went to the
shop and, having found the scroll, read it with care, followed the directions exactly, and persevered in the quest for a long time, but all his
efforts were unavailing till he gave up hope and besought God to help him.

[2] "Nearer than the neck-artery." See *Qur'ān* L, 15.

[3] For the meaning of simpleton (*ablah*) in this well-known Ḥadíth,
cf. Epistle to the Romans, XV, 19: "wise unto that which is good and
simple unto that which is evil." "Their foolishness," says Sulṭān Walad,
"is the highest wisdom: knowing nought of any but the Beloved, of
Him they are extremely conscious and aware."

XXXVII

THE MYSTIC WAY[1]

PLUG thy low sensual ear, which stuffs like
  cotton
Thy conscience and makes deaf thine inward ear.
Be without ear, without sense, without thought,
And hearken to the call of God, "*Return!*"
Our speech and action is the outer journey,
Our inner journey is above the sky[2]
The body travels on its dusty way;
The spirit walks, like Jesus, on the sea.

---

[1] *Math.* I, 566.
[2] The *introrsum ascendere* of medieval Christian mysticism.

XXXVIII

└─┐└─┐└─┐└─┐└─┐└─┐└─┐└─┐└─┐└─

THE SCEPTIC[1]

THE philosopher who disbelieves in the Moaning Pillar is
a stranger to the senses of the saints.[2]

He says the influence of melancholia brings many phantasies into people's minds.

Nay, this idle fancy of his is but the reflexion of his own
wickedness and infidelity.

He denies the existence of the Devil, and at the same time
he is possessed by a devil.

If thou hast not seen the Devil, behold thyself! Without
diabolic possession there is no blueness in the forehead.

Whosoever feels doubt in his heart is a secret philosopher.

He may profess firm belief, but some time or other that
philosophical vein will blacken his face for all to see.

Take care, O ye Faithful! That vein is in you: within you
is many an infinite world.[3]

Within you are all the two-and-seventy sects: woe to you if
one day they put forth their heads![4]

---

[1] *Math.* I, 3280.

[2] The miracle of the pillar (a palm-trunk in the Prophet's mosque at
Medina), against which he used to lean while preaching, is related in
Math. I, 2113 *seqq.* Subsequently a pulpit was set up for him, and when
he seated himself the deserted pillar "moaned and cried till it was
well-nigh split."

[3] *i.e.* conceptions and imaginations without end.

[4] The Prophet is said to have predicted that the Moslem community
would be divided into seventy-three sects, of which only one would
enter Paradise, the remainder being destined for Hell-fire.

XXXIX

THE EVIL IN OURSELVES[1]

THE Lion took the Hare with him: they ran together to
the well and looked in.

The Lion saw his own image: from the water appeared the
form of a lion with a plump hare beside him.

No sooner did he espy his enemy than he left the Hare and
sprang into the well.

He fell into the pit which he had dug: his iniquity recoiled
on his own head.

O Reader, how many an evil that you see in others is but
your own nature reflected in them!

In them appears all that *you* are—your hypocrisy, iniquity,
and insolence.

You do not see clearly the evil in yourself, else you would
hate yourself with all your soul.

Like the Lion who sprang at his image in the water, you
are only hurting yourself, O foolish man.

When you reach the bottom of the well of your own nature,
then you will know that the wickedness is in *you*.

---

[1] *Math.* I, 1306. In Rūmī's version of this Indian fable, the carnal
self (*nafs*) is represented as the lion who was lured by a hare to the
mouth of a deep well where, mistaking his own reflexion for a hated
rival, he sprang in and perished miserably. For the doctrine that all
so-called evil is an illusion arising from the diversity of Divine Attributes
—Beauty and Majesty, Mercy and Wrath, etc.—reflected in human
nature, and that only our egoism prevents us from seeing the "soul of
goodness" everywhere, cf. Nos. LXXXIX–XCV *infra*. So far as evil
exists in us, its source is the unreal "self" (*nafs*) by which we are separated from God. Purge the heart of "self," and evil disappears.

XL

THE HIERARCHY OF SAINTS[1]

In every epoch after Mohammed a Saint arises to act as
his viceregent: the people are on trial till the Resurrection.[2]

Whosoever has a good nature is saved, whosoever is of frail
heart is broken.

The Saint, then, is the living Imām, who appears in every
age, whether he be a descendant of 'Umar or of 'Alī.[3]

He is the God-guided one (Mahdī) and the Guide (Hādī):
he is both hidden and seated before you.[4]

He is as the Light of the Prophet, and Universal Reason is
his Gabriel: the saint lesser than he receives illumination from him, like a lamp.[5]

---

[1] *Math.* II, 815.

[2] The saying attributed to Mohammed, "there shall be no prophet
after me," was supplemented by Traditions concerning his spiritual
heirs and successors—a hierarchy ranged in classes of gradually increasing size under the supreme saint (*Quṭb*) of the age—who act as
touchstones whereby truth and falsehood are discriminated. So long as
the world endures, this process of testing (*āzmāyish*) will go on, and
whatever the hypocrite may profess, his attitude towards the Saints
will always betray his real character.

[3] Here the poet draws a sharp line between the Twelve Shī'ite
Imāms, descended from 'Alī (of whom the last vanished mysteriously
but is expected to reappear as the Mahdī at the end of the world) and
the uninterrupted succession of great Ṣūfī saints, who have no common
ancestry except their purely spiritual descent from the Prophet in virtue
of the "Light of Mohammed" (*Nūr-i Muḥammadī*) immanent in them all.

[4] The *Quṭb* is a "Mahdī" and a "Hidden Imām," but only in the
sense that he is the Divinely-guided Perfect Man who makes others
perfect (*Kāmil ū mukmil*), and that although seen by many he is recog-
nized by few.

[5] Having realized his essential unity with God, he transcends even
Universal Reason, the first individualization of the Absolute, just as
Mohammed in his Ascension left Gabriel behind at the moment when
he was about to enter the Divine presence (*Qur'ān* LIII). Probably the
"lamp" denotes one of the exalted saints known as *Abdāl* or *Awtād*.

77

The saint below this "lamp" is as the lamp-niche: the Light has gradations of intensity;[6]

For the Light of God has seven hundred veils: regard the veils of the Light as so many tiers.[7]

Behind each veil a certain class of saints has its abode: the veils mount tier after tier up to the Imām.

The light that is the life of the topmost rank is painful and insupportable to one beneath;

Yet, by degrees, his squintness diminishes; and when he has passed through all seven hundred veils, he becomes the Sea.[8]

The fire that is good for iron or gold—how should it be good for quinces and apples?

The apple and quince have only a slight crudity: unlike iron, they want a gentle heat;

But those flames are too mild for the iron, which easily absorbs the glow of the fiery dragon.

What is that iron? The self-mortified dervish: under the hammer and the fire he is red and happy.

He is the chamberlain of the fire, in immediate touch with it: he goes straight into the heart of the fire.

Therefore he is the Heart of the world, for by means of the heart the body performs its proper function.

All individual hearts are as the body in relation to the universal Heart of the Saint.

---

[6] "The lamp-niche" (*mishkāt*) alludes to a celebrated verse of the *Qur'ān* (XXIV, 35): "Allah is the Light of the heavens and the earth; the likeness of His Light is a niche wherein is a lamp."

[7] The Ḥadīth concerning seven hundred (or seventy thousand) veils of light and darkness which conceal the Face of Allah is expounded by Ghazālī in his *Mishkāt al-Anwār*. See Gairdner's translation, 88–98. The light-veils correspond to various degrees of saintship.

[8] "He becomes the Sea," *i.e.* he is completely submerged in the Essence. The following verses illustrate the inequality of spiritual capacity and endowment. The weaker brethren cannot dispense with the mediation of a Perfect Man inured to the fire of Divine Love, by which they themselves, if brought into direct contact with it, would be utterly destroyed before they were "cooked."

XLI

THE SPIRITUAL GUIDE[1]

THE Prophet said to 'Alī: "O 'Alī, thou art the Lion of
God, thou art a valiant knight,

But do not rely upon thy courage: come into the shadow
of the Palm-tree of hope.

Come into the shadow (protection) of the Sage whom none
can waylay.

His shadow on the earth is like Mt. Qāf, his spirit is like
the Sīmurgh that soars aloft.[2]

Though I should sing his praises until the Resurrection, do
not look for any end to them.

The Divine Sun has veiled Himself in Man: apprehend
this mystery, and God knows best what is the truth.

O 'Alī, above all works of devotion in the Way is the
shadow of God's Servant.[3]

When others seek to save themselves by religious works,

Go thou, take refuge in the shadow of the Sage against the
enemy within thee."

Having been accepted by the Pīr, give thyself up to him:
submit, like Moses, to the authority of Khizr.[4]

---

[1] *Math.* I, 2959. One of many passages in which the poet emphasizes
the need of saintly help and guidance for those who would take up arms
in "the greater Holy War" (*al-jihād al-akbar*) against the flesh, the world,
and the Devil.

[2] Qāf, the inaccessible mountain-range that is supposed to engirdle
the (flat) earth and said to be the home of the Sīmurgh, a mythical
bird which in Ṣūfism represents God or the soul regarded as a mode of
Divine Being.

[3] The Perfect Man, notwithstanding his virtual "deification," is
pre-eminently "God's Servant" (*'abdu 'llāh*), a title given to Mohammed
(*Qur'ān* LXXII, 19). He serves none other than God and has lost himself in the Object of his devotion.

[4] The unquestioning obedience which every Ṣūfī Shaykh demands
from his disciples is often illustrated by reference to the well-known

Whatever thy Khizr may do, bear it patiently, lest he say,
"Begone, *here we part*."

Though he scuttle the boat, be dumb! Though he kill a
child, do not tear thy hair!

God hath described his hand as His own, for He saith,
"*The Hand of God is over their hands*."[5]

This "Hand of God" slays his disciple, then brings him to
life everlasting.[6]

---

story of Khizr (Khaḍir) and Moses in *Qur'ān* XVIII, 64 *seqq.* Holy men
can justify all their actions, however incomprehensible and seemingly
immoral these may be.

[5] *Qur'ān* XLVIII, 10: "Verily, those who swear fealty to thee (the
Prophet) swear fealty to Allah: the Hand of Allah is over their hands."

[6] The *murshid*, acting as God's instrument, causes the disciple (*murīd*)
to die to self (*fanā*) and live in God (*baqā*).

XLII

THE USES OF TRIBULATION[1]

Look at a chickpea in the pot, how it leaps up when it is
subjected to the fire.

Whilst it is boiling, it always comes up to the top, crying
ceaselessly,

"Why are you setting the fire on me? You bought me:
why are you tormenting me like this?"

The housewife goes on hitting it with the ladle. "Now,"
says she, "boil nicely and don't jump away from her who
makes the fire.

I boil thee, but not because thou art hateful to me; nay,
'tis that thou mayst get savour

And become nutriment and mingle with the vital spirit:
such affliction is no abasement.

When thou wert green and fresh, thou drankest water in
the garden: that water-drinking was for the sake of this
fire.

God's mercy is prior to His wrath, to the end that by His
mercy thou mayst suffer tribulation.[2]

His mercy preceded His wrath in order that the stock-in-
trade, which is existence, should be produced;

For without pleasure flesh and skin do not grow, and unless
they grow, what shall Divine Love consume?

If, because of that requirement, acts of wrath come to pass
to the end that thou shouldst give up thy stock-in-trade,

---

[1] *Math.* III, 4159. The "housewife" is the *murshid*, the "chickpea"
the *murīd*, and the "fire" the Ṣūfī discipline of self-mortification.

[2] There are Traditions in which God declares that His mercy pre-
cedes or prevails over His wrath. Divine Love brought us into existence,
and its object cannot be realized without purging and transmuting our
fleshly qualities (*ṣifātu 'l-bashariyyah*).

81

Yet afterwards the Grace of God will justify them, saying 'Now thou art washed clean and hast jumped out of the river.'

Continue, O chickpea, to boil in tribulation until neither existence nor self remains to thee.

If thou hast been severed from the garden of earth, yet thou wilt be food in the mouth and enter into the living.[3]

Be nutriment, energy, thought! Thou wert milky sap: now be a lion of the jungle!

Thou grewest from God's Attributes in the beginning: pass again into His Attributes!

Thou wert a part of the cloud and the sun and the stars: thou wilt become soul and action and speech and thought.

The life of the animal arose from the death of the plant: hence the injunction, 'Slay me, O trusty friends,' is right.

Since such a victory awaits us after death, the words, 'Lo, in being slain I live,' are true."[4]

---

[3] In this and the following verses, spiritual evolution (see No. CXVIII *infra*) is symbolized by the process through which a chickpea, when cooked, eaten, assimilated, and converted into sperm, loses its vegetable nature, participates in the animal life of man, ascends to rationality, and eventually returns to the world of Divine Attributes from which it came.

[4] The words "slay me, O trusty friends" and "in being slain I live" are quoted from an Arabic ode by Ḥallāj, the most famous of Ṣūfī martyrs.

XLIII

"THE SPIRIT HELPETH OUR INFIRMITY"[1]

THE good thou art set upon, whate'er it be,
Its imperfection hath been hid from thee;
For were the vice laid bare, thy loathing soul
Would turn and fly from pole to farthest pole.
So, when an act of sin thou leav'st undone,
'Tis because God hath shown thee what to shun.[2]

O gracious Lord, with whom disguise is vain,
Mask not our evil, let us see it plain!
But veil the weakness of our good desire,
Lest we lose heart and falter and expire.

---

[1] *Math.* IV, 1332.
[2] Our evil thoughts and actions are the result of ignorance: they
would never come into being unless they were presented to us in the
form of good. God in His Wisdom lets appearances deceive us, so that
we sin blindly and remain in darkness till He opens our eyes.

XLIV

UNSEEN MIRACLES[1]

SECRET miracles and graces emanating from the Pīr
    transform the heart of the disciple;
For within the Saints there are spiritual resurrections
    innumerable, of which the least is this, that all nigh
    unto them become intoxicated with God.
If evidentiary miracles, like the Prophet's splitting of the
    moon, produce an immediate effect upon the soul,
'Tis because the soul is brought into touch with the Pro-
    ducer of the effect by means of a hidden link.
The effects which these miracles produce upon inanimate
    things are only accessory: their real object is invisible.
How superior is the bread made without dough—the
    Messiah's table of food from Heaven, Mary's fruit that
    never knew the orchard![2]

---

[1] *Math.* VI, 1300. Although it is the essential nature of all miracles
to bestow spiritual life, knowledge, and power on those who are capable
of being "converted," Rūmī makes a distinction in that respect between
the evidentiary miracle (*mu'jizah*) of the prophet and the secret miracle
(*karāmah*) of the saint. While the psychological effects of the *mu'jizah* are
associated with a manifest breach in the world-order, the miraculous
influence of the *murshid* on the *murīd* is a gift of Divine grace working
invisibly and directly in the heart.

[2] Analogies for faith that is "the substance of things unseen." See
Qur'ān III, 32 and V, 114.

XLV

THE REWARD OF THE RIGHTEOUS[1]

AT the Gathering for Judgement the Faithful will say, "O
   Angel, is not Hell the common road
Trodden by the believer and infidel alike? Yet we saw not
   any smoke or fire on our way."[2]
Then the Angel will reply: "That garden which ye saw as
   ye passed
Was indeed Hell, but unto you it appeared a pleasaunce of
   greenery.
Since ye strove against the flesh and quenched the flames
   of lust for God's sake,
So that they became verdant with holiness and lit the path
   to salvation;
Since ye turned the fire of wrath to meekness, and murky
   ignorance to radiant knowledge;
Since ye made the fiery soul (*nafs*) an orchard where
   nightingales of prayer and praise were ever singing—
So hath Hell-fire become for you greenery and roses and
   riches without end."

---

[1] *Math.* II, 2554.
[2] According to *Qur'ān* XIX, 72, all the Faithful shall enter Hell:
"there is not one of you but shall go down to it"—a text which is usually
interpreted as referring to the Bridge (*Şirāṭ*) over Hell. Cf. the Tradition
that Hell will speak to the Faithful on the Day of Judgement and say:
"Cross the Bridge, O true believer, for thy light hath put out my fire."

XLVI

THE SAINT'S VISION OF ETERNITY[1]

WHAT you see in the bright mirror—the Pīr sees more
than that in the unpolished iron brick.[2]

The Pīrs are they whose spirits were in the Sea of Divine
Munificence before this world existed.[3]

They lived ages before the creation of the body; they
harvested the wheat before it was sown.[4]

Before the form was moulded, they had received the spirit;
before the sea was made, they had strung the pearl.

The spirit has beheld the wine in the grape, the spirit has
beheld entity in non-entity—

The finite as infinite, the minted gold before the existence
of the mine.

---

[1] *Math.* II, 167.

[2] The "brick" (*khisht*) is the iron plate which the polisher (*ṣaqqāl*)
converts into a mirror. Where ordinary men perceive only the phenomenal aspect, the Pīr descries the real nature and character. As the
organ of Divine consciousness, "he knows the entire content of past,
present, and future existence, how everything came to be and is now
coming and shall at last come to be: all this he knows both synthetically
and analytically." (Jīlī.)

[3] *i.e.* they are universal modes (*ta'ayyunāt*) of Pure Being and essentially one with the Light of Mohammed (the Logos).

[4] The Perfect Man contemplates the final causes of things as logically
prior to their objective existence.

───┐ ───┐ ───┐ ───┐ ───┐ ───┐ ───┐ ───┐ ───┐ ───┐

XLVII

BEWARE OF HURTING THE SAINT[1]

O you who stab the selfless one with the sword, you are
stabbing yourself with it. Beware!

For the selfless one has passed away and is safe; he dwells
in safety for ever.

His form has passed away, he has become a mirror: naught
is there but the image of another's face.[2]

If you spit at it, you spit at your own face; and if you
strike the mirror, you strike yourself;

And if you see an ugly face in the mirror, 'tis you; and if
you see Jesus and Mary, 'tis you.

He is neither this nor that: he is pure and free from self:
he puts your image before you.

---

[1] *Math.* IV, 2138. These lines give the moral of a story concerning
Bāyazīd al-Bisṭāmī which the poet has borrowed, along with many
others, from the Legend of the Moslem Saints. It is related that one
day Bāyazīd, having attained to the state of "deification" cried out in
ecstasy, "Glory to me! Within this mantle there is none but God."
Rūmī describes the sequel:

"His disciples, frenzied with horror, dashed their knives at his holy
body,
Like the fanatics (Assassins) of Girdakūh, they ruthlessly stabbed
their spiritual Director.
Every one who plunged a dagger in the Shaykh made a gash in his
own body.
There was no wound on the body of the Master, while the disciples
were drowned in blood.
Whoever aimed a blow at his throat saw his own throat cut and
came to a miserable end."

[2] The perfect saint is the mirror of Truth, in which the real forms of
all things are reflected, good as good and evil as evil. Hence the poet
(II, 75) thanks God that in Ḥusāmu'l-Dīn he beholds nothing but
spiritual beauty and purity. If you are an enemy to the saints, it is only
because they show you the image of your hateful self.

XLVIII

THE DISINTERESTED CADI[1]

HE is God's deputy and the shadow of God's justice, the
mirror that displays the true nature of every plaintiff
and defendant;

For he inflicts punishment on behalf of those who have
been wronged; not for honour's sake nor in anger nor
for profit.

He who strikes and kills for his own sake is held responsible;
he who strikes and kills for God's sake is immune.

If a father beats his undutiful son and the son die in consequence, the father must pay the blood-price,[2]

Because he beat him for his own benefit: a son is bound to
serve his father.[3]

But suppose a schoolboy is flogged and dies: his teacher
incurs no penalty;

For it is not the boy's duty to serve his teacher: therefore
in chastising him he gains nothing for himself.[4]

The teacher is God's trustee; and the same rule applies to
every trustee.[5]

---

[1] *Math.* VI, 1512. Here the Perfect Man is depicted as a judge invested with superhuman authority and as a trustee responsible to God
alone.

[2] Abū Ḥanīfah was of this opinion.

[3] The son is bound to serve his father's interests: therefore the
father's motive in correcting the faults of his son is really self-interest,
and he incurs the legal penalty for manslaughter if his unsparing use of
the rod has fatal results.

[4] Moslem jurists hold that a teacher, acting as the deputy of Him
Who "taught Adam the Names," may inflict the most severe corporal
punishment on his pupils with impunity, since the benefit in this case is
entirely theirs.

[5] A trustee has no personal responsibility for unavoidable damage or
destruction of property placed in his charge.

Behead yourself! Whatever you do selflessly, 'tis a case of
thou didst not throw when thou threwest.[6]

---

[6] See *Qur'ān* VIII, 17. In reality it was God, not the Prophet, who
threw a handful of gravel in the faces of the Quraysh at Badr and
caused them to flee. Ṣūfīs frequently cite this text in connexion with
their doctrine of mystical self-abandonment (*fanā*).

XLIX

GOOD WORDS[1]

THE mother is always seeking her child: the fundamentals pursue the derivatives.

If water is confined in a tank, the wind sucks it up; for the wind is an elemental spirit, powerful and free.

It frees the water and wafts it away to its source, little by little, so that you cannot see it wafting;

And our soul likewise the breath of our praise steals away, little by little, from the prison of this world.

The perfumes of our good words ascend even unto Him, ascending from us whither He knoweth.[2]

Our breaths soar up with the choice words, as a gift from us, to the abode of everlastingness;

Then comes to us the recompense of our praise, a recompense manifold, from God the Merciful;

Then He causes us to seek more good words, so that His servant may win more of His Mercy.

Verily the source of our delight in prayer is the Divine Love which without rest draws the soul home.

---

[1] *Math.* I, 878. The "good words" (*al-kalim al-ṭayyiba*) are the Moslem profession of faith (*lā ilāha illā 'llāh*) and other expressions of praise and worship, used in the sense which Ṣūfīs attach to them.

[2] Cf. *Qur'ān* XXXV, 11.

L

"HERE AM I"[1]

ONE night a certain man cried "Allah!" till his lips grew
sweet with praising Him.

The Devil said, "O man of many words, where is the
response 'Here am I' (*labbayka*) to all this 'Allah'?

Not a single response is coming from the Throne: how long
will you say 'Allah' with grim face?"

He was broken-hearted and lay down to sleep: in a dream
he saw Khaḍir amidst the verdure,[2]

Who said, "Hark, you have held back from praising God:
why do you repent of calling unto Him?"

He answered. "No 'Here am I' is coming to me in response:
I fear that I am turned away from the Door."

Said Khaḍir, "Nay; God saith: That 'Allah' of thine is
My 'Here am I,' and that supplication and grief

And ardour of thine is My messenger to thee. Thy fear and
love are the noose to catch My Favour:

Beneath every 'O Lord' of thine is many a 'Here am I'
from Me."

---

[1] *Math.* III, 189. Selfless prayer arises from the presence of God in
the heart and is answered before it is uttered.

[2] The mysterious holy personage known by the name of Khaḍir
assumes many forms in Moslem legend. See the *Encyclopaedia of Islam.*
"Verdure" in this verse alludes to his name, literally "the green man,"
and his association with spiritual life and growth.

﹀﹀﹀﹀﹀﹀﹀﹀﹀﹀

LI

THE SOUL OF PRAYER[1]

JALALU'L-DÍN was asked, "Is there any way to God nearer than the ritual prayer?" "No," he replied; "but prayer does not consist in forms alone. Formal prayer has a beginning and an end, like all forms and bodies and everything that partakes of speech and sound; but the soul is unconditioned and infinite: it has neither beginning nor end. The prophets have shown the true nature of prayer. . . . Prayer is the drowning and unconsciousness of the soul, so that all these forms remain without. At that time there is no room even for Gabriel, who is pure spirit. One may say that the man who prays in this fashion is exempt from all religious obligations, since he is deprived of his reason. Absorption in the Divine Unity is the soul of prayer."[2]

---

[1] *Fīhi mā fīhi*, 15.

[2] Ṣūfīs often describe "the naughting of self-consciousness (*fanā'u 'l-ṣifāt*)" which results from intense concentration of every faculty on God in the performance of the ritual prayer (*ṣa'īt*). The Prophet is said to have declared that no *ṣalāt* is complete without the inward presence of God. To him every *ṣalāt* was a new Ascension (*mi'rāj*), in which he left even Gabriel behind. See *Kashf al-Maḥjūb*, p. 302.

LII

THE FRIEND WHO SAID "I"[1]

A CERTAIN man knocked at his friend's door: his friend asked, "Who is there?"

He answered, "I." "Begone," said his friend, "'tis too soon: at my table there is no place for the raw."

How shall the raw one be cooked but in the fire of absence? What else will deliver him from hypocrisy?

He turned sadly away, and for a whole year the flames of separation consumed him;

Then he came back and again paced to and fro beside the house of his friend.

He knocked at the door with a hundred fears and reverences, lest any disrespectful word might escape from his lips.

"Who is there?" cried his friend. He answered, "Thou, O charmer of all hearts!"

"Now," said the friend, "since thou art I, come in: there is no room for two I's in this house.

The double end of thread is not for the needle: inasmuch as thou art single, enter the needle."[2]

'Tis the thread that enters the needle: the needle's eye will not admit the camel.[3]

How shall the camel be fined down save by the shears of asceticism?[4]

---

[1] *Math.* I, 3056. Mystical union involves a transformation of the lover's personality into that of the Beloved.

[2] The mystic becomes "single" when he ceases to be conscious of himself as an *alter ego* beside God, who is the only real Ego.

[3] Unbelievers "will not enter Paradise till the camel passes through the needle's eye" (*Qur'án* VII, 38). Cf. St. Matthew XIX, 24.

[4] The carnal nature is symbolized by a thorn-eating camel.

But that, O reader, requires the Hand of God, which is the *Be and it was* of every impossibility.

Even non-existence, though more dead than the dead, must hearken when He calls it into being.

Recite the text, "*Every day He is engaged in some affair*: do not deem Him idle and inactive.[5]

His least act, every day, is that He despatches three armies:

One army from the loins of the fathers towards the mothers, in order that the plant may grow in the womb;

One army from the wombs to the Earth, that the world may be filled with male and female;

One army from the Earth to what lies beyond death, that every one may behold the beauty of good works.

---

[5] *Qur'ān* LV, 29.

LIII

┗━┓┗━┓┗━┓┗━┓┗━┓┗━┓┗━┓┗━┓┗━┓┗━┓

GOD BEYOND PRAISE[1]

WHEN beams of Wisdom strike on soils and
  clays
Receptive to the seed, Earth keeps her trust:
In springtime all deposits she repays,
Taught by eternal Justice to be just.

O Thou whose Grace informs the witless clod,
Whose Wrath makes blind the heart and eye
  within,
My praise dispraises Thee, Almighty God;
For praise is being, and to be is sin.[2]

---

[1] *Math.* I, 508. Everything in the universe obeys and glorifies God
(*Qur'ān* XVII, 46, etc.). Rūmī, like Ibnu'l-'Arabī, regards the whole
inanimate creation as potentially endowed with life, perception, knowledge and reason.
[2] These lines refer to the mystic's "passing away" from his praise of
God through absorption in the Object of praise (*al-fanā bi-'l-Madhkūr
'ani 'l-dhikr*). So long as he is certain of existing and acting individually,
he is in effect denying the Divine Unity. According to a hemistich
quoted by Junayd: "thy being (*wujūduka*) is a sin with which no other
sin may be compared."

LIV

KNOWLEDGE IS POWER[1]

KNOWLEDGE is the seal of the Kingdom of Solomon: the
   whole world is form, and knowledge is its spirit.[2]

Because of this virtue, the creatures of the seas and those
   of hill and plain are helpless before Man.

Of him the pard and the lion are afraid; the crocodile of
   the great river trembles.

From him peri and demon take refuge, each lurks in some
   hiding-place.

Man hath many a secret enemy: the cautious man is wise.

There are hidden beings, evil and good: at every moment
   their blows are falling on the heart.[3]

The pricks of angelic inspiration and satanic temptation
   come from thousands, not only from one.

Wait for your senses to be transmuted, so that you may
   discern these occult presences

And see whose words you have rejected and whom you
   have made your captain.

---

[1] *Math.* I, 1030.
[2] The phenomenal world is the outward form of Universal Reason;
its essence the Divine Knowledge that animates and rules it as the
spirit animates and rules the body. Man is potentially capable of attain-
ing to this knowledge, which may be likened to the magic seal whereby
Solomon exercised dominion over men and jinn and beasts and birds.
[3] A reference to the Moslem belief that the heart (*qalb*) is a battlefield for invisible hosts of devils and guardian angels.

LV

OUR REAL NAMES[1]

Do thou hear the name of every thing from the Knower:
hear the meaning of the mystery of *He taught him the
Names*.[2]

With us, the name of every thing is its outward form; with
the Creator, its inward essence.

In the eyes of Moses the name of his rod was "staff"; in
the eyes of God its name was "dragon."[3]

Here the name of 'Umar was "idolater"; but in eternity it
was "true believer."[4]

Before God, in short, that which is our end is our real
name.[5]

---

[1] *Math.* I, 1238.

[2] "The Knower," *i.e.* the possessor of immediate knowledge who,
like Adam (*Qur'ān* II, 29), receives it from God and sees all things as
they are in their essential nature.

[3] When Moses cast down his rod, it assumed the form of a dragon
from which Pharaoh's magicians and followers fled in panic.

[4] 'Umar, the second Caliph, before his conversion to Islam, was a
violent enemy of the Prophet and a persecutor of the Faithful.

[5] St. Francis of Assisi said, "What every one is in the eyes of God,
that he is, and no more."

⌣⌣⌣⌣⌣⌣⌣⌣⌣⌣⌣

IMMEDIATE KNOWLEDGE[1]

COME, recognize that your sensation and imagination and
understanding are like the reed-cane on which children ride.

The spiritual man's knowledge bears him aloft; the sensual
man's knowledge is a burden.

God hath said, *Like an ass laden with books*: heavy is the
knowledge that is not inspired by Him;[2]

But if you carry it for no selfish ends, the load will be lifted
and you will feel delight.[3]

How can you become free without the wine of Him,
O you who are content with the sign of Him?

From attribute and name what is born? Phantasy; but
phantasy shows the way to the Truth.[4]

Do you know any name without a reality? Or have you
ever plucked a rose from R.O.S.E.?[5]

You have pronounced the name: go, seek the thing named.
The moon is in the sky, not in the water.

Would you rise beyond name and letter, make yourself
entirely pure,

And behold in your own heart all the knowledge of the
prophets, without book, without learning, without
preceptor.

---

[1] *Math.* I, 3445.   [2] The quotation is from *Qur'ān* LXII, 5.
[3] *i.e.* God will endow you with real knowledge.
[4] Although the words denoting Divine Names and Attributes convey
but a shadowy idea (*khayāl*) of His nature, yet the Ṣūfī who recites them
and meditates on their meaning becomes inspired with love for their
object; for every Divine Name (*ism*) is ultimately identical with the Named
(*musammā*) whom it objectifies. Regarded externally it is only "the name of
a name" and constitutes a "veil" (*ḥijāb*) over the essence of the Named.
[5] For the doctrine that no appearance is altogether divorced from
reality, see No. XCV. "A rose from R.O.S.E.": in Persian, "*gul* from
(the letters) *gāf* and *lām*."

﹈﹈﹈﹈﹈﹈﹈﹈﹈﹈﹈

TRADITION AND INTUITION[1]

THE ear is a go-between, the eye a lover in unison with the
 beloved; the eye has the actual bliss, while the ear has
 only the words that promise it.[2]

In *hearing* there is a transformation of qualities; in *seeing*, a
 transformation of essence.[3]

If your knowledge of fire has been ascertained from words
 alone, seek to be cooked by fire!

There is no intuitive certainty until you burn: if you desire
 that certainty, sit down in the fire!

When the ear is subtle, it becomes an eye; otherwise, the
 words are enmeshed and cannot reach the heart.[4]

---

[1] *Math.* II, 858.

[2] The ear plays the part of a *dallālah* (professional match-maker),
whose business it is to describe a girl's beauty to the prospective bride-
groom.

[3] "Hearing" (*sam'*), *i.e.* knowledge based on authority, whether oral
or written, can change only the mental and moral qualities of the
hearer or reader: it cannot effect that complete transformation of the
"self" which is wrought by immediate vision of the Divine. In the next
verses Rūmī contrasts the certainty derived from "hearing" (*'ilmu 'l-
yaqīn*) with the certainty gained by seeing (*'aynu 'l-yaqīn*) and realized
in actual experience (*haqqu 'l-yaqīn*).

[4] The rudiments of spiritual knowledge are received through the ear,
and when these ideas penetrate the heart and are apprehended by the
oculus cordis, hearing becomes vision.

FEELING AND THINKING[1]

Some one struck Zayd a hard blow from behind. He was
about to retaliate,

When his assailant cried, "Let me ask you a question:
first answer it, then strike me.

I struck the nape of your neck, and there was the sound
of a slap. Now I ask you in a friendly way—

'Was the sound caused by my hand or by your neck,
O pride of the noble?'"

Zayd said, "The pain I am suffering leaves me no time to
reflect on this problem.

Ponder it yourself: he who feels the pain cannot think of
things like this."

---

[1] *Math.* III, 1380. An apologue showing the futility of intellectual
speculation in the face of mystical truth.

LIX

MYSTICAL PERCEPTION[1]

THE five spiritual senses are linked with one another: all the five have grown from one root.[2]

The strength of one invigorates the others: each becomes a cupbearer to the rest.

Vision increases the power of speech; the inspired speech makes vision more penetrating.

Clairvoyance sharpens every sense, so that perception of the unseen becomes familiar to them all.

When one sheep has jumped over a stream, the whole flock jump across on each other's heels.

Drive the sheep, thy senses, to pasture; let them browse in the verdant meadow of Reality,

That every sense of thine may become an apostle to others and lead all their senses into that Paradise;

And then those senses will tell their secret to thine, without words and without conveying either literal or metaphorical meanings.[3]

---

[1] *Math.* II, 3236.

[2] The faculties of the soul, corresponding to the five bodily senses, are derived from the Universal Spirit and serve to manifest Divine attributes: they are not separate and distinct but involved in one another. As Edward Carpenter says, "this (mystical) perception seems to be one in which all the senses unite into one sense."

[3] The illumined saint comes as an apostle to shed light on all and guide them to the Truth. He reads their hearts by pure intuition; his knowledge is infallible, since it is not communicated to him by words, which could only be ambiguous and misleading.

LX

LOVE AND FEAR[1]

THE mystic ascends to the Throne in a moment; the ascetic needs a month for one day's journey.

Although, for the ascetic, one day is of great value, yet how should his one day be equal to *fifty thousand years*?[2]

In the life of the adept, every day is fifty thousand of the years of this world.[3]

Love (*maḥabbat*), and ardent love (*'ishq*) also, is an Attribute of God; Fear is an attribute of the slave to lust and appetite.[4]

Love hath five hundred wings, and every wing reaches from above the empyrean to beneath the earth.

The timorous ascetic runs on foot; the lovers of God fly more quickly than lightning.

May Divine Favour free thee from this wayfaring! None but the royal falcon hath found the way to the King.

---

[1] *Math.* V, 2180, a passage contrasting the slow and painful progress (*sulūk*) of the self-centred ascetic with the inward rapture (*jadhbah*) which in a moment carries the mystic to his goal. Cf. No. XXV, note 3.

[2] From *Qur'ān* LXX, 4: "the angels and the Spirit (Gabriel) ascend to Him on a Day whereof the span is fifty thousand years." Ṣūfīs interpret this text as a reference to the mystical resurrection and ascension.

[3] "The life of the adept" consists entirely in contemplation (*mushā-hadah*), and its "days" (*ayyāmu 'llāh*) are the infinite, timeless epiphanies (*tajalliyāt*) in which God reveals Himself to His true lovers.

[4] There is Qur'ānic authority for *maḥabbat*, but none for *'ishq*, the key-word of Ṣūfī erotic symbolism. The stronger term, however, appears in a Holy Tradition reported by Ḥasan of Basrah (*ob.* A.D. 728): "God said, 'When My servant devotes himself to praise and recollection (*dhikr*) of Me and takes delight in it, I love him and he loves Me (*'ashi-qanī wa-'ashiqtuhu*).'"

LXI

THE ASCENDING SOUL[1]

I DIED as mineral and became a plant,
I died as plant and rose to animal,
I died as animal and I was Man.
Why should I fear? When was I less by
    dying?
Yet once more I shall die as Man, to soar
With angels blest; but even from angelhood
I must pass on: *all except God doth perish.*[2]
When I have sacrificed my angel-soul,
I shall become what no mind e'er conceived.
Oh, let me not exist! for Non-existence
Proclaims in organ tones. "To him we shall
    return."[3]

---

[1] *Math.* III, 3901. See Nos. CXVII and CXVIII.
[2] *Qur'ān* XXVIII, 88.
[3] *Qur'ān* II, 151. For the term "non-existence" (*'adam*) applied to self-abandonment (*fanā*), see No. CXIII, note 3.

LXII

THE NEGATIVE WAY[1]

IN the presence of the drunken Turk, the minstrel began
to sing of the Covenant made in eternity between God
and the soul.[2]

"I know not whether Thou art a moon or an idol, I know
not what Thou desirest of me,

I know not what service to do Thee, whether I should keep
silence or express Thee in words.

'Tis marvellous that Thou art Nigh unto me; yet where
am I and where Thou, I know not."

In this fashion he opened his lips, only to sing "I know not,
I know not."

At last the Turk leaped up in a rage and threatened him
with an iron mace.

"You crazy fool!" he cried. "Tell me something you know,
and if you don't know, don't talk nonsense."

"Why all this palaver?" said the minstrel, "My meaning
is occult."

Until you deny all else, the affirmation of God escapes

---

[1] *Math.* VI, 703.
[2] "Minstrel" probably denotes the Perfect Man teaching his disciples
to follow the path of self-negation (*fanā*), not as an end in itself, but
because it leads to positive and real union with God (*baqā*). In other
words, mystical "intoxication" (*sukr*) should be regarded only as a
prelude, and therefore relatively inferior, to "sobriety" (*saḥw*), in which
the mystic rises from negation of the Many to affirmation of the One
revealed in the Many. This is the true significance of the Moslem profession of faith, *lā ilāha illā 'llāh*, prefigured by the Primal Covenant
(*mīthāq*) in eternity between God and all human souls: "*He brought forth
from the children of Adam, from their reins, their seed, and made them testify of
themselves, saying, 'Am not I your Lord?' They answered, 'Yea, we testify.'*"
See *Qur'ān* VII, 171.

you: I am denying in order that you may find the way to affirm.

I play the tune of negation: when you die death will disclose the mystery—

Not the death that takes you into the dark grave, but the death whereby you are transmuted and enter into the Light.

O Amīr, wield the mace against yourself: shatter egoism to pieces!"

LXIII

THE SPIRIT OF THE UNIVERSE[1]

WHAT worlds mysterious roll within the vast,
The all-encircling ocean of the Mind!
Cup-like thereon our forms are floating fast,
Only to fill and sink and leave behind
No spray of bubbles from the Sea upcast.

The Spirit thou canst not view, it comes so nigh.[2]
Drink of this Presence! Be not thou a jar
Laden with water, and its lip stone-dry;
Or as a horseman blindly borne afar,
Who never sees the horse beneath his thigh.

---

[1] *Math.* I, 1109.
[2] Reason or Spirit, the Divine element in Man, is hidden from our perception by its immanence and the universality with which its attributes and effects are manifested.

LXIV

THE ABSOLUTE[1]

WE and our existences are non-existent: Thou art the
Absolute appearing in the guise of mortality.[2]

That which moves us is Thy Gift: our whole being is of Thy
creation.

Thou didst show the beauty of Being unto not-being, after
Thou hadst caused not-being to fall in love with Thee.[3]

Take not away the delight of Thy Bounty: take not away
Thy dessert and wine and wine-cup!

But if Thou take it away, who will question Thee? Does
the picture quarrel with the painter?

Look not on us, look on Thine Own Loving-kindness and
Generosity!

We were not: there was no demand on our part; yet Thy
Grace heard our silent prayer and called us into existence.[4]

---

[1] *Math.* I, 602. See the Introduction.

[2] Ibnu'l-'Arabī, and Rūmī after him, use the term "not-being" (*'adam*
or *nīstī*) to denote things which, though non-existent in one sense, are
existent in another: *e.g.* the external world, which exists as a form but
not as an essence, and the intelligible world, which exists as a concept
but not as a form.

[3] Here "not-being" signifies "relative non-existence," and is applied
to the world existing potentially as an idea in God's knowledge before
the latent realities (*a'yān-i thābitah*) of all things were brought into
actual and objective existence. God caused this "not-being" to love
Him, *i.e.* by His grace every "reality" (*'ayn-i thābitah*) or potentiality
was made capable (= desirous) of receiving the concrete existence which
He bestowed upon it.

[4] Existence (*wujūd*) is a Divine Gift and, like all the Gifts of God, is
conferred "on request." The request (*su'āl*) may be either explicit or
implicit, *i.e.* in virtue of the state or capacity of the asker, as, for example,
the state of a parched plant amounts to a request for water, while a seed

In the Divine court of audience all are helpless as tapestry
before the needle.
Now He makes a portrait of the Devil, now of Adam; now
He depicts joy, now sorrow.
None can raise a hand in defence; none dare utter a word
concerning injury or benefit.

---

buried in the earth is virtually *asking* to grow and spring up. From this
point of view, "everything was created at the demand of need"
(*Math.* III, 3204 *seqq.*).

LXV

⌣⌣⌣⌣⌣⌣⌣⌣⌣

FONS VITAE[1]

Poor copies out of Heaven's original,
Pale earthly pictures mouldering to decay,
What care although your beauties break and
    fall,
When that which gave them life endures for
    aye?

Oh, never vex thine heart with idle woes:
All high discourse enchanting the rapt ear,
All gilded landscapes and brave glistering
    shows
Fade—perish, but it is not as we fear.

Whilst far away the living fountains ply,
Each petty brook goes brimful to the main.
Since brook nor fountain can for ever die,
Thy fears how foolish, thy lament how vain!

What is this fountain, wouldst thou rightly
    know?
The Soul whence issue all created things.
Doubtless the rivers shall not cease to flow
Till silenced are the everlasting springs.

Farewell to sorrow, and with quiet mind
Drink long and deep: let others fondly deem

---

[1] *Dīwān, SP,* XII.

The channel empty they perchance may find,
Or fathom that unfathomable stream.

The moment thou to this low world wast given,
A ladder stood whereby thou mightst aspire;
And first thy steps, which upward still have
    striven,
From mineral mounted to the plant; then
    higher

To animal existence; next, the Man
With knowledge, reason, faith. O wondrous
    goal!
This body, which a crumb of dust began—
How fairly fashioned the consummate whole!

Yet stay not here thy journey: thou shalt grow
An angel bright and have thine home in Heaven.
Plod on, plunge last in the great Sea, that so
Thy little drop make oceans seven times seven.

"The Son of God!" Nay, leave that word
    unsaid;
Say, "God is One, the pure, the single Truth."
What though thy frame be withered, old, and
    dead,
If the soul keep her fresh immortal youth?

LXVI

THE PURPOSE OF CREATION[1]

DIVINE Wisdom created the world in order that all things
in His Knowledge should be revealed.

God laid upon the world the throes of parturition for the
purpose of making manifest that which He knew.[2]

You cannot sit inactive for a moment, you cannot rest till
some good or evil has issued from you.

All these cravings for action were ordained to the end that
your inward consciousness should come clearly into sight.

How can the real, which is the body, be at rest when the
thread, which is the mind, is pulling it?[3]

This world and yonder world are incessantly giving birth:
every cause is a mother, its effect the child.

When the effect is born, it too becomes a cause and gives
birth to wondrous effects.

These causes are generation on generation, but it needs a
very well lighted eye to see the links in their chain.

---

[1] *Math.* II, 994.

[2] God has willed that the world, of which Man is the epitome, should
objectify the whole content of His Knowledge. Our ceaseless activities
arise from the duty of manifesting the Divine consciousness which is the
ground of human nature.

[3] Since God is always working in the heart, the body cannot be idle.
"The tree of Man was never quiet."

LXVII

DIVINE PROVIDENCE[1]

Does any painter paint a beautiful picture for the sake of
the picture itself?

Nay, his object is to please children or recall departed
friends to the memory of those who loved them.

Does any potter mould a jug for the jug's sake and not in
hope of the water?

Does any calligrapher write for the writing's sake and not
for the benefit of the reader?

'Tis like moves in chess, my son: perceive the result of
each move in the next one.

By discerning cause within cause, one after another, you
arrive at victory and checkmate.

The man of dull spirit knows not how to advance: he acts
on trust and steps forward blindly.

Blind trust, when you are engaged in war, is as vain as a
gambler's reliance on his luck.[2]

When the barriers in front and behind are lifted, the eye
penetrates and reads the tablet of the Invisible.

Such a clairvoyant looks back to the origin of existence—
he sees the angels dispute with the Almighty as to making
our Father (Adam) His vicegerent;[3]

---

[1] *Math.* IV, 2881.

[2] In the battle against the flesh those who have no light but from
their own wits inevitably lose the game.

[3] *Qur'ān* II, 28: "The Lord said to the angels, 'Lo, I am about to
place a viceroy in the earth.' They said, 'Wilt Thou place therein one
who will do evil and shed blood? (We are more worthy, since) we
glorify Thee.' God said, 'Verily I know what ye know not.' "

And again, casting his eye forward, he beholds all that shall come to pass till the Day of Judgement.

Everyone sees the things unseen according to the measure of his illumination.

The more he polishes the heart's mirror, the more clearly will he descry them.

Spiritual purity is bestowed by the Grace of God; success in polishing is also His Gift.

Work and prayer depend on aspiration: *Man hath nothing but what he hath worked for.*[4]

God alone is the Giver of aspiration: no churl aspires to be a King;[5]

Yet God's assignment of a particular lot to any one does not hinder him from exercising will and choice.

When trouble comes, the ill-fated man turns his back on God, while the blessed man draws nigher unto Him.

---

[4] *Qur'ān* LIII, 40.
[5] The mystic's aspiration is the consequence and proof of his pre-election.

LXVIII

CAUSATION[1]

GOD hath established a rule and causes and means for the sake of all who seek Him under this blue canopy.

Most things come to pass according to the rule, but sometimes His Power breaks the rule.

He established a goodly rule and custom: He made the evidentiary miracle a breach of the custom.

O thou who art ensnared by causes, do not imagine that the Causer is defunct!

The Causer brings into existence whatsoever He will, His Omnipotence can destroy all causes;

But, for the most part, He lets the execution of His Will follow the course of causation, in order that seekers may be able to pursue their object of desire.

When there is no cause, what way should the seeker pursue? He must have a visible cause in the way he is going.

Causes are films on the eyes, for not every eye is worthy to contemplate His work.

It needs a piercing eye to reach beyond the cause and remove the film entirely,

So as to behold the Causer in the spaceless world and see that all our exertion and action is mere drivel.[2]

---

[1] *Math.* V, 1543. Divine Action transcends the apparent correlation of cause and effect which serves to maintain the world-order by providing a basis for human activities.

[2] This vision of the seer is not inconsistent with the view that devotional works are Divinely appointed *means* of approach to Reality (No. XXXII). What renders them worthless is our failure to discern the immediate operation of Divine Grace in creating and giving effect to them, if it be His Will so to do.

Everything good or bad comes from the Causer: causes and means, O father, are naught

But a spectre that has appeared on the King's highway in order that the reign of ignorance may endure for a little while.

LXIX

THE DIVINE FACTORY[1]

THE Worker is hidden in the workshop: enter the workshop and behold Him!

Inasmuch as the work has woven a veil over the Worker,
you cannot see Him outside of His work.[2]

The Worker dwells in the workshop: none who stays outside is aware of Him.

Come, then, into the workshop of Not-being, that you may
contemplate the work and the Worker together.[3]

Pharaoh set his face towards material existence; therefore
he was blind to God's workshop

And wished to alter and avert that which was eternally
ordained.

---

[1] *Math.* II, 759.

[2] God's work is the actualization of the potential. The worker in the
immaterial world perpetually clothes "not-being" with His Qualities.

[3] By dying to self (*fanā*) the mystic returns, as it were, to his pre-
existent state of "not-being" as an *'ayn-i thābitah* and realizes the inseparable unity of the Divine Essence, Attributes, and Actions.

LXX

⌐⌐⌐⌐⌐⌐⌐⌐⌐⌐

THE WORLD OF TIME[1]

Every instant thou art dying and returning. "This world
is but a moment," said the Prophet.

Our thought is an arrow shot by Him: how should it stay
in the air? It flies back to God.

Every instant the world is being renewed, and we unaware
of its perpetual change.

Life is ever pouring in afresh, though in the body it has the
semblance of continuity.[2]

From its swiftness it appears continuous, like the spark
thou whirlest with thy hand.

Time and duration are phenomena produced by the
rapidity of Divine Action,

As a firebrand dexterously whirled presents the appearance of a long line of fire.

---

[1] *Math.* I, 1142. The circle of existence begins and ends in a single
point, the Essence of God, which is perceived by us under the form of
extension. To mystics, however, the world is "but a moment," *i.e.* a
flash of Divine illumination revealing the One as the Many and the
Many as the One. According to Ṣūfī and other Moslem metaphysicians,
every atom of the Cosmos is continually annihilated and re-created by
the immediate manifestation of Divine Energy.

[2] Cf. the saying of Heraclitus, "To him who enters the same river,
other and still other waters flow."

LXXI

REALITY AND APPEARANCE[1]

'Tis light makes colour visible: at night
Red, green, and russet vanish from thy sight.
So to thee light by darkness is made known:
All hid things by their contraries are shown.
Since God hath none, He, seeing all, denies
Himself eternally to mortal eyes.[2]

From the dark jungle as a tiger bright,
Form from the viewless Spirit leaps to light.
When waves of thought from Wisdom's Sea profound
Arose, they clad themselves in speech and sound.
The lovely forms a fleeting sparkle gave,
Then fell and mingled with the falling wave.
So perish all things fair, to re-adorn
The Beauteous One whence all fair things were born.

---

[1] *Math.* I, 1121. The symbolism of light and colour comes originally from Plato.
[2] Having no object to compare and contrast with God, the mind cannot apprehend Him: it perceives only the diverse forms in which He appears.

LXXII

⌐⌐⌐⌐⌐⌐⌐⌐⌐⌐

GOD IN NATURE[1]

THE world is frozen: its name is *jamād* (inanimate): *jāmid*
  means "frozen," O master.

Wait till the rising of the sun of Resurrection, that thou
  mayst see the movement of the world's body.[2]

Since God hath made Man from dust, it behoves thee to
  recognize the real nature of every particle of the universe,

That while from this aspect they are dead, from that aspect
  they are living: silent here, but speaking Yonder.

When He sends them down to our world, the rod of Moses
  becomes a dragon in regard to us;[3]

The mountains sing with David, iron becomes as wax in
  his hand;[4]

The wind becomes a carrier for Solomon, the sea understands what God said to Moses concerning it.[5]

The moon obeys the sign given by Mohammed, the fire (of
  Nimrod) becomes a garden of roses for Abraham.[6]

They all cry, "We are hearing and seeing and responsive,
  though to you, the uninitiated, we are mute."

---

[1] *Math.* III, 1008.

[2] At the Resurrection, *i.e.* when, either here or hereafter, God lets us
see things as they really are, we shall know the material world in its
inward aspect, which is the world of spirit and everlasting life.

[3] *Qur'ān* VII, 104 *seqq.*

[4] *Qur'ān* XXI, 79; XXXIV, 10.

[5] The wind was subject to Solomon (*Qur'ān* XXI, 81) and trans-
ported his throne from one country to another. God said to Moses,
"Smite the sea with thy rod" (*Qur'ān* XXVI, 63), whereupon it opened
a way for the Israelites but engulfed Pharaoh and his hosts.

[6] This verse refers to the splitting of the moon (*Qur'ān* LIV, 1) and
to the miraculous preservation of Abraham (*Qur'ān* XXI, 69).

Ascend from materiality into the world of spirits, hearken
   to the loud voice of the universe;
Then thou wilt know that God is glorified by all inanimate
   things: the doubts raised by false interpreters will not
   beguile thee.[7]

---

[7] According to the *Qur'ān* (XVII, 46), "there is not a thing in heaven
or earth but glorifies Him." While for Ṣūfīs *taṣbīḥ-i jamādāt* is a Divinely
revealed truth as well as a fact of mystical experience, Moslem ration-
alistic theologians explain that such praise of God can only be implicit
or indirect: *e.g.* the sight of a mineral or plant may cause the person
contemplating it to cry *subḥān Allāh!*

⌣⌐ ⌣⌐ ⌣⌐ ⌣⌐ ⌣⌐ ⌣⌐ ⌣⌐ ⌣⌐ ⌣⌐ ⌣⌐

LXXIII

AMOR AGITAT MOLEM[1]

Love is a boundless ocean, in which the heavens are but a flake of foam.

Know that all the wheeling heavens are turned by waves of Love: were it not for Love, the world would be frozen.

How else would an inorganic thing change into a plant? How would vegetive things sacrifice themselves to become endowed with (the animal) spirit?[2]

How would (the animal) spirit sacrifice itself for the sake of that Breath by the waft whereof a Mary was made pregnant?[3]

All of them would be stiff and immovable as ice, not flying and seeking like locusts.

Every mote is in love with that Perfection and mounts upward like a sapling.

Their silent aspiration is, in effect, a hymn of Glory to God.

---

[1] *Math.* V. 3853.

[2] See Nos. LXI and CXVIII.

[3] The elect are inspired and regenerated by the Divine Spirit which was breathed into the Virgin Mary (*Qur'án* XXI, 91; LXVI, 12). Cf. *Fíhi má fíhi*, 22: "The body is like Mary, and every one of us hath a Jesus within. If the pains (of love) arise in us, our Jesus will be born." This recalls Eckhart's doctrine of the birth of Christ in the soul (Inge, *Christian Mysticism*, 162 *seq.*) and especially his saying, "The Father speaks the Word into the soul, and when the 'son' is born every soul becomes Mary."

LXXIV

UNIVERSAL LOVE:[1]

NEVER, in sooth, does the lover seek without being sought
by his beloved.[2]

When the lightning of love has shot into *this* heart, know
that there is love in *that* heart.

When love of God waxes in thy heart, beyond any doubt
God hath love for thee.

No sound of clapping comes from one hand without the
other hand.

Divine Wisdom in destiny and decree made us lovers of one
another.

Because of that fore-ordainment every part of the world is
paired with its mate.

In the view of the wise, Heaven is man and Earth woman:
Earth fosters what Heaven lets fall.

When Earth lacks heat, Heaven sends it; when she has lost
her freshness and moisture, Heaven restores it.

Heaven goes on his rounds, like a husband foraging for the
wife's sake;

And Earth is busy with housewiferies: she attends to births
and suckling that which she bears.

Regard Earth and Heaven as endowed with intelligence,
since they do the work of intelligent beings.

Unless these twain taste pleasure from one another, why
are they creeping together like sweethearts?

---

[1] *Math.* III, 4393. Divine Love pervades the Cosmos which it created.
All things, however diverse they may seem, are ruled by that essential
principle and moved to work in common for its fulfilment.

[2] If Love desires Beauty, no less does Beauty desire Love: see the
closing lines of the passage.

Without the Earth, how should flower and tree blossom?
What, then, would Heaven's water and heat produce?

As God put desire in man and woman to the end that the
world should be preserved by their union,

So hath He implanted in every part of existence the desire
for another part.

Day and Night are enemies outwardly: yet both serve one
purpose,

Each in love with the other for the sake of perfecting their
mutual work.

Without Night, the nature of Man would receive no in-
come, so there would be nothing for Day to spend.

The soul says to her base earthly parts, "My exile is more
bitter than yours: I am celestial."

The body desires green herbs and running water, because
its origin is from those;

The soul desires Life and the Living One, because its
origin is the Infinite Soul.

The desire of the soul is for ascent and sublimity; the
desire of the body is for pelf and means of self-indulgence;

And that Sublimity desires and loves the soul: mark the
text *He loves them and they love Him*.[3]

The gist is that whenever any one seeks, the soul of the
sought is desiring him;

But the lover's desire makes him haggard, while the loved
one's desire makes him fair and comely.

Love, which brightens the beloved's cheek, consumes the
soul of the lover.

The amber loves the straw with the appearance of wanting
naught, while the straw is struggling to advance on the
long road.

---

3 *Qur'ān* V, 59. What attracts lover to beloved and *vice versa*, and
harmonizes and unites them, is nothing that exists in the phenomenal
world: it is the "non-existent" Essence and Reality which mystics know
by the name of Love. In the beloved it appears under the aspect of
lordship and self-sufficiency, in the lover it takes the form of servitude,
abasement and tribulation.

LXXV

MAN THE MACROCOSM[1]

From the pure star-bright souls replenishment is ever
coming to the stars of heaven.

Outwardly we are ruled by these stars, but our inward
nature has become the ruler of the skies.[2]

Therefore, while in form thou art the microcosm, in reality
thou art the macrocosm.

Externally the branch is the origin of the fruit; intrinsically
the branch came into existence for the sake of the fruit.

Had there been no hope of the fruit, would the gardener
have planted the tree?

Therefore in reality the tree is born of the fruit, though it
appears to be produced by the tree.

Hence Mohammed said, "Adam and all the prophets
march behind me under my banner."[4]

---

[1] *Math.* IV, 519.

[2] Heaven derives its light from the Divine Attributes which illumine
the spirit of the Perfect Man. Cf. Ibn u'l-Fāriḍ: "My moon never sinks,
my sun is never hidden, and all the radiant stars set their course by
me."

[3] The theory of Moslem philosophers that the universe is a great
Man and Man a little universe requires correction. According to Ṣūfīs,
Man, though he may be regarded as a microcosm, is not a mere epitome
of the universe: on the contrary, he is its origin and final cause, since it
was brought into existence for his sake, and essentially the Perfect Man
is the spirit of Divine Revelation through whom the whole purpose of
creation is fulfilled. Cf. the verses ascribed to 'Alī:

"Thou art the perspicuous Book whose letters unravel all mysteries.
Thou deemest thyself a small body (microcosm), yet the greater
world (macrocosm) is enfolded within thee."

[4] All the prophets were inspired by the Light of Mohammed, who
(speaking as the Logos) is said to have declared that he was a prophet
when Adam was clay.

Hence that Master of every lore uttered the mystic saying,
  "We are the hindmost and the foremost:"[5]
That is to say, "If seemingly I am born of Adam, yet in
  truth I am the ancestor of every ancestor.
Since the angels worshipped him for my sake, and he
  ascended to the Seventh Heaven on my account,
Therefore Father Adam was really born of me: the tree
  was born of the fruit.
The idea, which is first, comes last into actuality, in parti-
  cular the idea that is eternal."

---

[5] This Tradition asserts the superiority of Islam to Judaism and
Christianity, but here Rūmī gives it a mystical turn. Mohammed, the
last of the prophets in time, is the first of them in eternity.

LXXVI

‿⁊‿⁊‿⁊‿⁊‿⁊‿⁊‿⁊‿⁊‿⁊‿⁊

THE PERFECT MAN[1]

THE Quṭb is the lion: it is his business to hunt: all the rest
eat his leavings.

So far as you can, endeavour to satisfy him, so that he may
gain strength and hunt the wild beasts.[2]

When he is ailing, the people starve: all food comes from
the hand of Reason.

Their spiritual experiences are only his leavings. Bear this
in mind, if you desire the prey.

He is like Reason, they are as members of the body; the
management of the body depends on Reason.[3]

His infirmity is of the body, not of the spirit: the weakness
lies in the Ark, not in Noah.

The Quṭb revolves round himself, while round him revolve
all the spheres of Heaven.

Lend some assistance in repairing his bodily ship: be his
chosen slave and devoted servant.

In reality your aid is a benefit to you, not to him: God
hath said, "If ye help God, ye will be helped."[4]

---

[1] *Math.* V, 2339. The term *Quṭb* (Pole), as used here, denotes the
Perfect Man generally and does not refer specifically to the Head of the
Ṣūfī hierarchy.

[2] "Endeavour to satisfy him," *i.e.* "serve him faithfully, relieve his
bodily wants, and take care not to disturb him, so that he may be left
free to pursue the realities (*asrār ū maʿānī*) which are his spiritual food.
That this is what Rūmī means by "the wild beasts" cannot be doubted.
Giordano Bruno in his allegory of Actaeon (*The Heroic Enthusiasts*, tr.
Williams, vol. I, p. 91) not only employs the same phrase but explains
it as signifying "the intelligible kinds of ideal conceptions, which are
occult, followed by few, visited but rarely, and which do not disclose
themselves to all those who seek them."

[3] The Quṭb, being "the form of Universal Reason," is the manager
(*mudabbir*) of the world. Without his mediation, it would not be spiritually fed. See No. LXVIII.   [4] *Qurʾān* LXVII, 8.

LXXVII

‿‿‿‿‿‿‿‿‿‿

THE WITNESS TO GOD[1]

GOD hath not created in the earth or in the lofty heaven
 anything more occult than the spirit of Man.

He hath revealed the mystery of all things, moist and dry,
 but He hath sealed the mystery of the spirit: *"it is of the
 Word of my Lord."*[2]

Since the august eye of the Witness beheld that spirit,
 naught remains hidden from him.

God is named "the Just," and the Witness belongs to Him:
 the just Witness is the eye of the Beloved.[3]

The object of God's Regard in both worlds is the pure
 heart: the King's gaze is fixed upon the favourite.

The mystery of His amorous play with His favourite was
 the origin of all the veils which He hath made.[4]

Hence our Loving Lord said to the Prophet on the night of
 the Ascension: "But for thee I would not have created
 the heavens."

---

[1] *Math.* VI, 2877.

[2] *Qur'ān* XVII, 87.

[3] The Perfect Man's relation to God is analogous to that of an incor-
ruptible eye-witness whose evidence determines the judgement and thus
brings into clear light the justice and other invisible qualities of the
judge.

[4] The phenomenal world was created in order that the Perfect Man
might be evolved and the glory of Divine Love fully displayed in him.
He, therefore, is the Beloved of God (*Ḥabību 'llāh*), a title pre-eminently
belonging to Mohammed.

LXXVIII

THE MEDIATOR[1]

THE Prophet said, "God doth not regard your outward
forms: therefore in your devising seek ye the owner of
the Heart."[2]

'Tis by His Favour God regards thee, not because of thy
prostrations in prayer and thy almsgivings.

Since thou deemest hearts like thine to be the Heart, thou
hast abandoned the search for those who possess it—

The Heart into which if seven hundred Heavens should
enter, they would be lost and hidden from view.

Do not call such fragments of heart as these "the Heart":
do not seek an Abū Bakr in Sabzawār![3]

The owner of the Heart is a six-faced mirror: through him
God looks on all the six directions.[4]

If God reject any one, 'tis for his sake; and if He accept
any one, 'tis on his authority.

God lays His Bounty on the palm of his hand, and his
palm dispenses it to all objects of Divine Mercy.

The oneness of Universal Mercy with his palm is unquali-
fied and unconditional and perfect.

---

[1] *Math.* V, 869.

[2] "The owner of the Heart," *i.e.* the saint. For "heart" (*dil, qalb*) as
a name for the organ of spiritual perception, cf. *oculus cordis* in Western
mysticism.

[3] Here the poet alludes to a story (*Math.* V, 845 *seqq.*) concerning the
people of Sabzawār (Bayhaq), who were so fanatically Shī'ite that no
Sunnī could live among them.

[4] "The six directions": right, left, above, below, before, behind. The
Perfect Man is "the eye of the world whereby God sees His own works"
and becomes conscious of Himself in all his diverse aspects.

O rich man, if thou bring to God a hundred sacks of gold,
  He will say, "Bring the Heart as a gift to My door:[5]
Bring Me the Heart that is the Pole of the world and the
  Soul of the soul of the soul of Adam!"

---

[5] Referring to *Qur'ān* XXVI, 83-89: "on the Day when riches and
sons avail not (and none shall be helped) save him who bringeth unto
God a sincere heart (*qalb salīm*)."

ASCETICISM AND GNOSIS[1]

THE gnostic is the soul of religion and piety; gnosis is the result of past asceticism.[2]

Asceticism is the labour of sowing; gnosis is the growth and harvesting of the seed.

The gnostic is both the command to do right and the right itself; both the revealer of mysteries and that which is revealed.[3]

He is our King to-day and to-morrow: the husk is for ever a slave to his goodly kernel.

---

[1] *Math.* VI, 2090.

[2] "Result," *i.e.* essential substance and final cause.

[3] Since the Perfect Man unites in his consciousness all inward and outward aspects of Reality, it may be said that he is at once the Law and the Law-giver, the Mystery and the Hierophant.

LXXX

⌐_⌐_⌐_⌐_⌐_⌐_⌐_⌐_⌐_⌐_⌐_

"DIE BEFORE DEATH"[1]

THE Prophet said, "O seeker of the mysteries, wouldst thou see a dead man living,

Walking on the earth, like living men; yet his spirit dwells in Heaven,

Because it has been translated before death and will not be translated when he dies—

A mystery beyond understanding, understood only by dying—

If any one wish to see a dead man walking thus visibly on the earth,

Let him behold Abū Bakr, the devout, who in virtue of being a true witness to God became the Prince of the resurrected."[2]

Mohammed is the twice-born in this world: he died to all temporal losing and finding: he was a hundred resurrections here and now.[3]

----

[1] *Math.* VI, 742. The famous saying, *mūtū qabla an tamūtū*, is one of a very large number which Ṣūfīs attribute to the Prophet as evidence for their claim to have inherited his esoteric doctrine. In the following verses Rūmī paraphrases and expounds a Tradition enjoining the Faithful to imitate Abū Bakr, a type of the perfect saint dead (*fānī*) to the world and living (*bāqī*) in God. Not only Abū Bakr, but 'Umar, 'Uthmān, and 'Alī, are included among the prophets and holy men by whom the pre-existent "Light of Mohammed" is transmitted from generation to generation (*Math.* II, 905–930; cf. No. LXXXVIII).

[2] "A true witness to God": see No. LXXVII. Abū Bakr is well-known by the title of *al-Ṣiddīq*.

[3] In the Islamic world the Prophet's Ascension represents the supreme mystical experience of the "resurrected" soul which has become one with him.

131

Often they would ask him, "How long is the way to the
Resurrection?"[4]

And he would answer with mute eloquence, "Does any one
ask that of me who am the Resurrection?"[5]

Become the Resurrection and so behold it: becoming is the
necessary condition for beholding the reality of anything.

Whether it be light or darkness, until thou become it thou
wilt never know it completely.

---

[4] On being asked this question, the Prophet is said to have answered,
raising his forefinger and middle finger together, "I and the Resurrection are as these twain."

[5] "With mute eloquence," literally "with the tongue of the inward
state (ḥāl)." According to Rūmī, the Prophet did not *say* "I am the
Resurrection" (cf. St John XI, 25: ἐγώ εἰμι ἡ ἀνάστασις καὶ ἡ ζωή)
but let his essential nature speak for itself.

LXXXI

MYSTICAL DEATH AND BURIAL[1]

THY sepulchre is not beautified by means of stone and
wood and plaster;[2]

Nay, but by digging for thyself a grave in spiritual purity
and burying thy egoism in His Egoism

And becoming His dust and buried in love of Him, so that
His Breath may fill and inspire thee.

A tomb with domes and turrets is unpleasing to followers of
the Truth.

Look now on a living man attired in satin: does the superb
robe help his understanding at all?

His soul is tormented, the scorpion of anguish dwells in his
sorely stricken heart.[3]

Outside, broideries and decorations; but within he is
moaning, a prey to bitter thoughts;

And lo, another, wearing an old patched cloak, his thoughts
sweet as the sugar-cane, his words like sugar!

---

[1] *Math.* III, 130.
[2] The body resembles a tomb: to build it up and adorn it with the
gauds of this world is a bad preparation for happiness hereafter.
[3] Scorpions are supposed to infest the graves of infidels and evil-doers
till the Resurrection.

⌐⌐⌐⌐⌐⌐⌐⌐⌐⌐

UNITY OF SPIRIT[1]

WHEN the rose is dead and the garden ravaged, where
shall we find the perfume of the rose? In rose-water.

Inasmuch as God comes not into sight, the prophets are
His vicars.

Do not mistake me! 'Tis wrong to think that the vicar
and He Whom the vicar represents are two.

To the form-worshipper they are two; when you have
escaped from consciousness of form, they are One.

Whilst you regard the form, you are seeing double: look,
not at the eyes, but at the light which flows from them.[2]

You cannot distinguish the lights of ten lamps burning together, so long as your face is set towards this light alone.

In things spiritual there is no partition, no number, no
individuals.

How sweet is the oneness of the Friend with His friends!
Catch the spirit and clasp it to your bosom.

Mortify rebellious form till it wastes away: unearth the
treasure of Unity!

Simple were we and all one essence: we were knotless and
pure as water.[3]

---

[1] *Math.* I, 672, a discourse on the Divine vicegerency (*Khilāfah*) of
the prophets, in whom the hidden nature of God is revealed.

[2] Dualism is the result of paying attention to the outward forms of
things. As the eyes are two, but their light one and indistinguishable, so
the bodies of the prophets are many, but the spirit which illumines them
one and the same. Moslem oculists generally adopt the theory of Galen
and other Greeks that vision is produced by rays of light emitted from
the eyes.

[3] Ṣūfīs identify the so-called "White Pearl," the spiritual essence of
Man and original substance of all created things, with the Light of
Mohammed (Universal Reason, the Logos).

When that goodly Light took shape, it became many, like
shadows cast by a battlement.

Demolish the dark battlement, and all difference will
vanish from amidst this multitude.[4]

---

[4] "The dark battlement" typifies the wall of selfhood and illusion, to
which the "shadows" of plurality owe their existence.

⌣⌐⌣⌐⌣⌐⌣⌐⌣⌐⌣⌐⌣⌐⌣⌐⌣⌐⌣⌐

LXXXIII

CREATIONS OF PHANTASY[1]

O THOU by Whom the unspoken prayer is answered,
Who bestowest at every moment a hundred bounties on
the heart.

Thou hast limned some letters of writing: rocks here
become soft as wax for love of them.[2]

Thou hast scribed the *nūn* of the eyebrow, the *ṣād* of the eye
and the *jīm* of the ear as a distraction to our minds and
understandings.[3]

By those letters of Thine the intellect is made to weave
subtle coils of perplexity: write on, O accomplished
Fair-writer!

Incessantly Thou shapest beauteous forms of phantasy
upon the page of Non-existence.

On the tablet of phantasy Thou inscribest wondrous letters
—eye and profile and cheek and mole.

I am drunken with desire for Non-existence, not for the
existent, because the Beloved of the world of Non-
existence is more faithful.[4]

---

[1] *Math.* V, 309.

[2] The Platonist, William Drummond, uses the same analogy:

> "Those golden letters which so brightly shine
> In Heaven's great volume gorgeously divine,
> The wonders all in sea, in earth, in air
> Be but dark pictures of that sovereign Fair."

[3] The Arabic letters *ṣād*, *nūn*, and *jīm* resemble in shape the eye, the
eyebrow, and the ear respectively. Viewed in its proper light, everything in the world is good. But where mystics, contemplating these
"fair copies," whether sensible or ideal, perceive only the revelation of
Eternal Beauty in ever-changing forms of "new creation," other men
see and pursue mere shadows of their selfish selves.

[4] "Non-existence," *i.e.* Reality as opposed to phenomenality.

Behold how the madmen dote on the blackness of those lines traced without fingers!

Everyone is infatuated with a phantasy and digs in corners for the buried treasure.

One goes into church to perform religious exercises; another in his greed for gain betakes himself to sowing;

One loses his soul in the invocation of demons; another sets his foot upon the stars.

To the seeing eye it is manifest that all variety of action in the external world arises from phantasies within.

Since the object of the soul's quest is hidden, every one looks for it in a different quarter, like travellers seeking the *qiblah* in the dark.

At dawn, when the Ka'bah becomes visible, they find out who has lost his way.[5]

---

5 As a rule, the ritual prayer (*ṣalāt*) is invalidated by facing in the wrong direction, but should the worshipper, owing to darkness or any other sufficient cause, fail to turn towards the Ka'bah, he does not lose the merit of his prayers, provided that he has endeavoured to the best of his judgement and ability to ascertain the direction as exactly as possible. Similarly all seek the One True Light (No. CIV). Doubt, perplexity, and error arise from ignorance.

⌐⌐⌐⌐⌐⌐⌐⌐⌐⌐

THE MAGIC OF LOVE[1]

Love and fancy create a thousand forms beautiful as Joseph: in sooth they are greater sorcerers than Hārūt and Mārūt.[2]

Before your eyes they raise up the phantom of the Beloved: you are enraptured with it and tell it all your secrets.

'Tis as when a mother, at the grave of her child newly dead,

Speaks to him earnestly and intensely: crazed with grief, she imagines his dust to be living

And in her heart believes he is listening to her. Lo, the magic wrought by Love!

Fondly and with tears she lays her lips, time after time, on the fresh earth of the grave in such wise

As, during his life, she never laid them on the face of the son who was so dear to her.

But love for the dead does not last: when some days have passed in mourning, the flame of her grief sinks to rest.

Love has carried off his enchantments and gone away: the fire is out, only ashes remain.

---

[1] *Math.* V, 3260.

[2] Two fallen angels who taught mankind the arts of magic. Presuming themselves to be immaculate, they had refused to do homage to Adam, so God sent them down to the earth, where they fell in love with a beautiful woman and tried to seduce her. She would not yield until they taught her the word of power that enabled them to ascend to Heaven. Having learned it, she ascended, and God transformed her into Zuhrah (the planet Venus). Hārūt and Mārūt were imprisoned in a pit at Babylon, choosing to expiate their sin in this world rather than suffer everlasting torment hereafter. The legend may be regarded as an allegory of the human spirit and reason, which descend from the World of Light to the World of Nature, fall a prey to the defilements of the flesh (*nafs*), and finally, having been purged by suffering, return to where they belong.

LXXXV

PHENOMENA THE BRIDGE TO REALITY[1]

THE Christian confesses to his priest a year's sins—forni-
cation and malice and hypocrisy—
In order that the priest may pardon him, for he deems the
priest's absolution to be forgiveness from God.
The priest has no real knowledge of sin and pardon; but
love and faith are mighty spells.

In the hour of absence Love fashions many a form of
phantasy; in the hour of presence the Formless One
reveals Himself,
Saying, "I am the ultimate origin of sobriety and intoxication: the beauty in all forms is reflected from Me.
Now, because thou hast often gazed on My reflexion, thou
art able to contemplate My Pure Essence."

As soon as the Christian feels the pull from Yonder, he
becomes unconscious of the priest.
At that moment he craves forgiveness for his trespasses
from the Grace of God behind the veil.
When a fountain gushes from a rock, the rock disappears
in the fountain.

---

[1] *Math.* V, 3257 and 3277.

﹈﹈﹈﹈﹈﹈﹈﹈﹈﹈

THE PEAR-TREE OF ILLUSION[1]

THIS pear-tree is the primal egoism and self-existence that
makes the eye distorted and squinting.

When thou comest down, O climber, thy thoughts and
words and eyes will no more be awry.

Because of the humility shown by thee in coming down,
God will endow thee with true vision.

Thou wilt see that this pear-tree has become a tree of
fortune, its boughs reaching to the Seventh Heaven.

Afterwards climb up again into the tree transformed by
Divine Mercy.

Now it is luminous like the Burning Bush: it cries, *"Lo, I
am God!"*[2]

Beneath its shade all thy wants are satisfied: such is the
Divine Alchemy.

Thy personality and existence are now lawful to thee, since
thou beholdest therein the attributes of the Almighty.

The crooked tree has become straight, God-revealing:
its root in the earth, its branches in the sky.[3]

---

[1] *Math.* IV, 3562. Boccaccio (*Decameron*, Day vii, Novel 9) and
Chaucer in *The Merchant's Tale* relate how a gallant, by climbing a
pear-tree and pretending that it caused hallucinations, persuaded the
foolish husband to believe in his wife's innocence, though he had witnessed her misbehaviour with his own eyes. Rūmī's version of the story
is given in the preceding couplets (3544–3557). Here he draws out of it
a mystical application—the soul's "climb-down" from self-consciousness
and ascent to God-consciousness—which goes far to justify his sometimes
very broad interpretation of the maxim that every jest has a moral.

[2] See *Qur'ān* XXVIII, 29–30, and cf. Exodus III, 1–6.

[3] *Qur'ān* XIV, 29.

COSMIC CONSCIOUSNESS[1]

WINE in ferment is a beggar suing for our ferment; Heaven
in revolution is a beggar suing for our consciousness.

Wine was intoxicated with us, not we with it; the body
came into being from us, not we from it.

We are as bees, and bodies as the honeycomb: we have
made the body, cell by cell, like wax.[2]

---

[1] *Math.* I, 1811. Here the poet speaks as one of the God-intoxicated
souls which live in union with the Logos and therefore may claim to be
the archetype and animating principle of the universe.

[2] As bees by Divine inspiration (*Qur'ān* XVI, 70-71) build up
honeycombs, so the Spirit of the Perfect Man makes the world an image
of itself and fills all bodies, according to the capacity of each, with
sweetness and light and knowledge and love of God.

LXXXVIII

THE UNIVERSAL SPIRIT
REVEALED IN PROPHETS
AND SAINTS[1]

EVERY moment the robber Beauty rises in a different
shape, ravishes the soul and disappears.

Every instant the Loved One assumes a new garment, now
of eld, now of youth.

Now He plunged into the heart of the potter's clay—the
Spirit plunged like a diver.[2]

Anon, rising from the depths of clay that is moulded and
baked, He appeared in the world.

He became Noah, and went into the Ark when at His
prayer the world was flooded.

He became Abraham and appeared in the midst of the fire,
which bloomed with roses for His sake.[3]

For a while He was roaming on the earth to pleasure
Himself;

Then He became Jesus and ascended to Heaven and
glorified God.

In brief, it was He that was coming and going in every
generation thou hast known,

Until at last He appeared in the form of an Arab and
gained the empire of the world.

There is no transmigration, nothing is transferred. The
lovely Winner of hearts

---

[1] *Dīwān, Tab.*, 199.
[2] The Divine Spirit was breathed into the clay body of Adam, which
God had kneaded with His own hands for forty days.
[3] See No. LXXII, note 6.

Became a sword in the hand of 'Alī and appeared as the
Slayer of the time.[4]

No, no! 'Twas even He that cried in human shape, "*Ana
'l-Ḥaqq.*"

The one who mounted the scaffold was not Manṣūr, as the
foolish imagined.[5]

Rūmī hath not spoken and will not speak words of infidelity: do not disbelieve him!

---

[4] Here Rūmī explicitly warns the reader against confusing a monistic
doctrine with the heresy of those who believe in the transmigration of
individual souls (*tanāsukh*). In another passage (*Dīwān*, Lucknow ed.,
p. 222) he declares that all forms in which the One Essence clothes itself
are "different bottles of the same Wine," and "this," he says, "is not
transmigration: it is the doctrine of Pure Unity" (*īn nīst tanāsukh, sukhun-i
waḥdat-i ṣirf-ast*).

[5] "Manṣūr" refers to Ḥallāj (Ḥusayn ibn Manṣūr) executed at
Baghdad in A.D. 922. He expressed his mystical relation to God in the
emphatic formula *Ana 'l-Ḥaqq*, "I am God," but he would not have
endorsed Rūmī's interpretation of it. Cf. No. CXV.

LXXXIX

THE STANDARD-BEARERS OF
DIVINE REVELATION[1]

THE eternal Will and Decree of God, the Forgiver, to
reveal and manifest Himself

Invokes opposition, for otherwise nothing can be shown;
and there is no contrary to that incomparable King.[2]

Therefore He made a viceroy whose heart should be a
mirror for His Sovereignty,

And endowed him with infinite purity, and then set up
against him a dark foil.

He made two banners, white and black: one was Adam,
the other was Iblīs.

Between these mighty hosts there was combat and strife,
and there came to pass what was destined to come.

Likewise in the next period Abel arose, and Cain became
the antagonist of his pure light.

So, from age to age and from generation to generation, the
same banners were raised in conflict,

Till the advent of Mohammed, who strove with Abū Jahl,
the prince of the armies of iniquity.

---

[1] *Math.* VI, 2151.
[2] The manifestation of God in the world evokes the appearance of
contrariety; hence in successive ages His Beautiful and Terrible Attributes are personified and displayed as antagonists contending for
mastery, though *essentially* they are one as He is One.

XC

THE MYSTERY OF EVIL[1]

BOTH Moses and Pharaoh were worshippers of the Truth, though in appearance the former has found the way and the latter has lost it.[2]

In the daytime Moses was crying to God: at midnight Pharaoh would begin to moan,[3]

Saying, "O Lord, what shackle is this on my neck? Were there no shackle, who would say 'I am I'?[4]

By that decree whereby Thou hast made Moses to be illumined, by that same decree Thou hast made me to be darkened.

Both of us are fellow-slaves to Thee; but Thy axe is cleaving the sappy boughs in Thy forest.

The boughs are helpless against the axe: one it grafts firmly, another is left uncared for.

I beseech Thee, by the might of Thine axe, to show mercy and straighten my crookedness."

Once more Pharaoh said to himself in amazement, "Am not I praying all night long?

Within I am humble and obedient: how do I appear so changed when I meet with Moses?"[5]

---

[1] *Math.* I, 2447.

[2] Pharaoh no less than Moses serves the purpose for which he was created. It follows that *sub specie aeternitatis* all souls are ultimately saved.

[3] Moses worshipped God openly. Pharaoh, on the other hand, while proclaiming his own divinity in public, secretly acknowledged his absolute dependence on the Almighty, *i.e.* his original nature testified that he was a "vessel of wrath" and that his impiety was in accord with the inscrutable Divine Will and Knowledge concerning him.

[4] Early Ṣūfī authors quote the saying (repeated by Eckhart), "None but God has the right to say 'I'."

[5] Pharaoh's actions faithfully reflected his nature and character as it existed potentially in the Divine Mind, so that in essence there was

Since colourlessness became captive to colour, a Moses
came into conflict with a Moses.

When you attain unto the colourlessness which you had
originally, Moses and Pharaoh are at peace with one
another.[6]

If you ask me to explain this mystery, I reply that the
world of colour cannot be devoid of opposition.

The marvel is that colour sprang from that which is without
colour: how did colour arise to war with the colourless?

Or is it not really war? Is it for Divine ends—an artifice
like the bickering of ass-dealers?[7]

Or is it neither this nor that? Is it sheer bewilderment?
The treasure must be sought, and bewilderment is the
ruin where it lies buried.[8]

---

complete harmony between him and God; he only became hostile when
confronted with Moses, who represents the Command (*amr*) of God as
revealed to the prophets and embodied in the religious law. What God
commands is entirely good; but what He *wills* includes all "good" and
"evil," though nothing is really evil in relation to Him.

[6] "Colourlessness," the realm of pure being and absolute unity, in
which there is no "colour," *i.e.* individualization (*ta'ayyun*) or limitation
of any kind. Cf. Shelley:

> "Life, like a dome of many-coloured glass,
> Stains the white radiance of eternity."

"Colour" also suggests the dyeing-vat of Destiny and the various
characters that emerge from it. When the one appears as the Many,
"a Moses comes into conflict with a Moses," *i.e.* the Unity displays itself
in forms which, though outwardly opposed, are in fact nothing but the
Divine Essence viewed under the aspect of "otherness" and, like water
and ice, ultimately identical.

[7] Does not all this show of discord mark a deep design and har-
monious purpose? Wrangling ass-dealers are engaged in a conspiracy
to deceive the customer and incite him to buy.

[8] Or, again, is the creation of the world a riddle insoluble by the
intellect? May not the key be found in mystical bewilderment? Treasures
are buried in ruins: the treasure of Divine Unity (*tawḥīd*) is discovered
only by those "unbuilt from the creature" (Suso), "denuded (*verwues-
te*) of all attributes, empty (*wueste*) of themselves and of all things"
(Eckhart).

What you conceive to be the treasure—any such conception
causes you to lose the real treasure.

Fancies and opinions are like the state of cultivation:
treasure is not found in cultivated spots.

In the state of cultivation there is existence and contrariety: the Non-existent spurns everything that exists.[9]

---

[9] "The Non-existent," *i.e.* the formless Reality.

‿‿‿‿‿‿‿‿‿‿

THE LAW AND THE TRUTH[1]

YESTERDAY a man who was fond of dialectic put a question to me.

He said, "The Prophet says that to be pleased with infidelity is an act of infidelity; and his words are conclusive, like a seal.

But he has also declared that the Moslem must be pleased with every Divine Ordainment.

Now, is not infidelity and hypocrisy God's Ordainment? If I am pleased with infidelity, I shall be disobeying God,

And if I am not pleased, that too will be wicked: how can I escape from this dilemma?"

I replied, "Infidelity is the thing ordained: not the Ordainment, but the effect of the Ordainment.[2]

I acquiesce in infidelity in that respect that it is God's Ordainment, not in this respect that it is our rebelliousness and wickedness.

In respect of the Ordainment, infidelity is not infidelity. Do not call God "infidel," recant!

---

[1] *Math.* III, 1362.

[2] Acceptance of the Divine Decree (*qaḍā*) does not necessitate acceptance of the thing decreed (*maqḍī*). It is true that all sins are decreed by God; but He decrees them *quâ* actions, all of which in their essential nature proceed from Himself and are approved by Him, *not* as objects of condemnation on religious grounds. There is only an apparent conflict between His *creative* command, which brings every action into existence, and His *religious* command, which qualifies some actions as good and others as evil. The religious command is really a trial of faith and may be either obeyed or disobeyed. Therefore, while we are bound to condemn what is sinful in the eyes of the Law, we must at the same time acknowledge that God decrees and creates what, though He and we call it "sin," is in perfect unison with His Eternal Wisdom and Providence.

Infidelity is ignorance, and the Ordainment of infidelity is wisdom: how, pray, should *ḥilm* (ruth) and *khilm* (wrath) be identical?

The ugliness of the script is not the ugliness of the scribe; nay, 'tis an exhibition of the ugly by him.

The power of the artist is shown by his ability to make both the ugly and the beautiful.

If I develop this topic, so that question and answer become lengthy,

The savour of Love's mystery will go from me, the fair form of Piety will be disfigured.

XCII

THE COMPLETE ARTIST[1]

He is the source of evil, as thou sayest,
Yet evil hurts Him not. To make that evil
Denotes in Him perfection. Hear from me
A parable. The heavenly Artist paints
Beautiful shapes and ugly: in one picture
The loveliest women in the land of Egypt
Gazing on youthful Joseph amorously;
And lo, another scene by the same hand,
Hell-fire and Iblīs with his hideous crew:
Both master-works, created for good ends,
To show His Perfect Wisdom and confound
The sceptics who deny His Mastery.
Could He not evil make, He would lack skill:
Therefore He fashions infidel alike
And Moslem true, that both may witness bear
To Him, and worship One Almighty Lord.[2]

---

[1] *Math.* II, 2535.
[2] While the Divine Beauty and Mercy reflected in the nature of true believers cause them to worship God for love's sake, infidels are dominated by His Majesty and Wrath and only against their will confess themselves to be His slaves (*'ibād*).

XCIII

⌣,⌣,⌣,⌣,⌣,⌣,⌣,⌣,⌣,⌣

THE NECESSARY FOIL[1]

PRIVATION and defect, wherever seen,
Are mirrors of the beauty of all that is.
The bone-setter, where should he try his skill
But on the broken limb? The tailor where?
Not, surely, on the well-cut finished coat.
Were no base copper in the crucible,
How could the alchemist his craft display?

---

[1] *Math.* I, 3201. The nature of everything is made manifest by contrast with something else that lacks its qualities. Were there no appearance of darkness and evil, we should be ignorant of light and good. To be conscious of deficiency is the first step towards perfection.

THE RELATIVITY OF EVIL[1]

THERE is no absolute evil in the world: evil is relative. Recognize this fact.

In the realm of Time there is nothing that is not a foot to one and a fetter to another.

To one a foot, to another a fetter; to one a poison, to another sweet and wholesome as sugar.

Snake-venom is life to the snake, but death to man; the sea is a garden to sea-creatures, but to the creatures of earth a mortal wound.

Zayd, though a single person, may be a devil to one and an angel to another:

If you wish him to be kind to you, then look on him with a lover's eye.

Do not look on the Beautiful with your own eye: behold the Sought with the eye of the seeker.

Nay, borrow sight from Him: look on His face with His eye.

God hath said, "Whoso belongs to Me, I belong to him: I am his eye and his hand and his heart."

Everything loathly becomes lovely when it leads you to your Beloved.[2]

---

[1] *Math.* IV, 65.

[2] In this and the preceding verse the poet refers to three Traditions. He who gives himself up entirely to God (in *fanā*) is united with Him (in *baqā*). "Paradise is encompassed with things we like not," *i.e.* we must pass through tribulations in order to reach it.

XCV

⌐⌐⌐⌐⌐⌐⌐⌐⌐⌐

THE SOUL OF GOODNESS IN
THINGS EVIL[1]

Fools take false coins because they are like the true.
If in the world no genuine minted coin
Were current, how would forgers pass the false?
Falsehood were nothing unless truth were there,
To make it specious. 'Tis the love of right
Lures men to wrong. Let poison but be mixed
With sugar, they will cram it into their mouths.
Oh, cry not that all creeds are vain! Some scent
Of truth they have, else they would not beguile.
Say not, "How utterly fantastical!"
No fancy in the world is all untrue.
Amidst the crowd of dervishes hides one,
One true fakir. Search well and thou wilt find!

---

[1] *Math.* II, 2928. Error, falsehood and all evil is relative in so far as it serves to make truth and goodness manifest and is sought, not for itself, but only because it is mistaken for good. Cf. the argument of Socrates (*Meno* 77, tr. Jowett): "They do not desire the evils, who are ignorant of their nature, but they desire what they suppose to be goods although they are really evils; and if they are mistaken and suppose the evils to be goods, they really desire goods."

XCVI

THE UNSEEN POWER[1]

WE are the flute, our music is all Thine;
We are the mountain echoing only Thee;
Pieces of chess Thou marshallest in line
And movest to defeat or victory;
Lions emblazoned high on flags unfurled—[2]
Thy wind invisible sweeps us through the world.

---

[1] *Math.* I, 599.
[2] This was a sight the poet must often have witnessed during his residence at Qoniyah. Banners and coins bearing the device of a lion surmounted by a sun are associated with the Seljūq dynasties of 'Irāq and Asia Minor.

~⌐~⌐~⌐~⌐~⌐~⌐~⌐~⌐~⌐~

MORAL RESPONSIBILITY[1]

IF we let fly an arrow, the action is not ours: we are only
the bow, the shooter of the arrow is God.

This is not compulsion (*jabr*): it is Almightiness (*jabbārī*)
proclaimed for the purpose of making us humble.[2]

Our humbleness is evidence of Necessity, but our sense of
guilt is evidence of Free-will.

If we are not free, why this shame? Why this sorrow and
guilty confusion and abashment?

Why do masters chide their pupils? Why do minds change
and form new resolutions?

You may argue that the asserter of Free-will ignores God's
Compulsion, which is hidden like the moon in a cloud;

But there is a good answer to that: hearken, renounce
unbelief, and cleave to the Faith!

When you fall ill and suffer pain, your conscience is awakened, you are stricken with remorse and pray God to
forgive your trespasses.

The foulness of your sin is shown to you, you resolve to
come back to the right way;

You promise and vow that henceforth your chosen course
of action will be obedience.

Note, then, this principle, O seeker: pain and suffering

---

[1] *Math.* I, 616. Rūmī defends the orthodox Moslem doctrine that
"the creature does not create his actions and is not forced: God creates
these actions together with the creature's having a free choice (*ikhtiyār*)
in them."

[2] God calls Himself the Compeller (*al-Jabbār*) in order to remind us
that we are His slaves and entirely subject to His Will.

make one aware of God; and the more aware one is, the
greater his passion.[3]

If you are conscious of God's Compulsion, why are you not
heart-broken? Where is the sign of your feeling the
chains with which you are loaded?

How should one make merry who is bound in chains?
Does the prisoner behave like the man who is free?

Whatever you feel inclined to do, you know very well that
you can do it;

But in the case of actions that you dislike, you have become
a Necessitarian, saying, "Such is God's Decree."

The prophets are Necessitarians as regards the works of this
world; the infidels are Necessitarians as regards the
works of the world hereafter.

---

[3] Suffering causes the sinner to repent, and true penitence implies
self-abandonment, *i.e.* knowledge and love of God. Hence the Necessitarian, if he were really conscious of being "compelled," would turn to
God in anguish and supplication like a distraught lover.

⌣ ，⌣ ，⌣ ，⌣ ，⌣ ，⌣ ，⌣ ，⌣ ，⌣ ，⌣

"WHATSOEVER GOD WILLS SHALL COME TO PASS"[1]

THIS does not mean that you may be slack in serving God;
nay, 'tis an incitement to eager exertion and entire
self-devotion.

Suppose you knew that the will of such and such a vizier
is law and his munificence unbounded,

Would you pay court to him with the zeal of a hundred
men, or would you flee from him and his palace?

Likewise the Prophet's saying, "The Pen has dried," when
you interpret it in its true sense, is a summons to the
most important work of all.

If you do iniquity, you are damned: the Pen has dried on
that. If you act righteously, you will eat the fruit of
blessedness: the Pen has dried on that.

Is it conceivable that because of the Decree in eternity God
should say, like a minister dismissed from office,

"The affair has gone out of My hands: 'tis vain to approach
Me with entreaties"?

Nay, if your orisons exceed those of another by a single
mite, that mite will be weighed in God's scales.[2]

----

[1] *Math.* V, 3111.
[2] Cf. *Qur'ān* XCIX, 7.

PREDESTINATION AND FREE-
WILL¹

A Moslem called a Magian to accept the Faith of the
Prophet. He replied, "I shall do so, if God will."

"God wills it," said the Moslem; "but your carnal soul
and the wicked Devil are dragging you to infidelity and
the fire-temple."

"Well," he answered, "if they are the stronger, must not I
go in the direction whither they pull me?

You say that God desires me to profess Islam: what is the
use of His Desire when He cannot fulfil it?

According to you, the Flesh and the Devil have carried
their will to success, while the gracious Divine Purpose
has been defeated and pulverized.²

God forbid! Whatsoever He wills shall come to pass. He
is the Ruler over the worlds of space and spacelessness.

Without His Command no one in His Kingdom shall add
so much as the tip of a single hair.

The Kingdom is His, the Command is His: that Devil of
His is the meanest dog at His door."

"Beyond doubt," replied the Moslem, "we possess a certain

---

¹ *Math.* V, 2912. In the long-drawn debate from which a few extracts
are given here, the Magian upholds absolute necessitarianism, while the
Moslem declares such a doctrine to be absurd.

² The same argument was used by an eminent Ṣūfī, Abū Sulaymān
Dārānī (*ob.* A.D. 830), against the Qadarites and Muʿtazilites: "they
have made themselves and the Devil stronger than God; for they say
that He created His creatures to obey Him and that Iblīs converted
them to disobedience. Thus they maintain that when they will a thing
it comes to pass, but when God wills a thing it does not come to pass."

power of choice: you cannot deny the plain evidence of
the inward sense.

There is such a power of choice in regard to injustice and
wrong-doing: that is what I meant when I spoke of the
Flesh and the Devil.3

The instinct to choose is latent in the soul, and sight of the
desired object brings it into action.

When Iblīs shows to you an object of desire, the sleeping
power awakes and moves towards it,

While, on the other hand, the Angel sets before you good
objects of desire and commends them to your heart,

In order that the power to resist evil and choose good may
be stimulated."

In the eyes of reason, Necessitarianism (*jabr*) is worse than
the doctrine of absolute free-will (*qadar*), because the
Necessitarian is denying his own consciousness.4

The other does not deny this, he denies the action of the
Almighty: he says, "There is smoke, but no fire."5

The Necessitarian sees the fire plainly: it burns his raiment,
and like the sceptic he argues that it is naught.6

"If none but God has the power of choice, why are you
angry with a thief who steals your property?

Even animals recognize this inward sense: a camel, cruelly

---

3 Although the Moslem, speaking the language of religion, attributed
the Magian's infidelity to these evil forces, he did not mean that their
operation is irresistible: on the contrary, it is limited by a faculty in
man which enables him to choose whether or no he will accept the
temptation offered to him.

4 The existence of that which is beyond perception can more reasonably be denied than the existence of that which is perceived by the outward or inward senses. Consequently, from this point of view, the Jabrī,
who denies his manifest power of choice (*ikhtiyār*) is worse than the
Qadarī (Mu'tazilite), who denies the invisible Divine action.

5 *i.e.* he perceives the effect (*athar*), namely his free-will, but imputes
it to himself, ignoring the Creator and Producer of the effect (*Mu-
'aththir*), on Whose Will his choice of good or evil ultimately depends.

6 The Jabrī is a thorough-going sceptic, for he contradicts a universal fact of human consciousness.

159

beaten, attacks the driver; his fury is not directed against the cudgel.

The entire *Qur'ān* consists of commands and prohibitions and threats of punishment: are these addressed to stones and brickbats?

You have removed from God the possibility of impotence, but you have virtually called Him ignorant and stupid.

The doctrine of Free-will does not imply Divine impotence; and even if it did, ignorance is worse than impotence.

God's universal power of choice brought our individual power into existence: His Power is like a horseman hidden by the dust which he raises;

But His control of our acts of free-will does not deprive them of that quality.

Declare that God's Will is exercised in a complete manner, yet without imputing to Him compulsion (*jabr*) and responsibility for disobedience to His Commands.

You say your unbelief is willed by Him: know that it is also willed by yourself;

For without your will it cannot exist at all: involuntary unbelief is a self-contradiction.

Endeavour to gain inspiration from God's cup of love: then you will become selfless and without volition.

Then all volition will belong to that Wine, and you will be absolutely excusable."

C

THE WINE OF LOVE[1]

HE comes, a Moon whose like the sky ne'er saw,
    awake or dreaming,
Crowned with eternal flame no flood can lay.
Lo, from the flagon of Thy love, O Lord, my soul
    is swimming,
And ruined all my body's house of clay.

When first the Giver of the grape my lonely heart
    befriended,
Wine fired my bosom and my veins filled up;
But when His image all my eye possessed, a voice
    descended:
"Well done, O sovereign Wine and peerless Cup!"

Love's mighty arm from roof to base each dark
    abode is hewing
Where chinks reluctant catch a golden ray.
My heart, when Love's sea of a sudden burst into
    its viewing,
Leaped headlong in, with "Find me now who may!"

    As, the sun moving, clouds behind him run,
    All hearts attend thee, O Tabrīz's Sun!

---

[1] *Dīwān, SP.* VII.

CI

THE RIDDLES OF GOD[1]

WHOSOEVER is perplexed and sorely troubled, God hath
  whispered a riddle into his ear,

That He may enmesh him in two doubtful thoughts—
  "Shall I do what He tells me or shall I not?"

By God's Decree one of these alternatives tilts the scale,
  and he adopts it.

Wouldst thou have a mind untroubled, do not stuff thy
  spiritual ear with cotton-wool,

So that thou mayest understand His riddles and read both
  the covert sign and the overt.

Then upon thine ear will descend revelation (*waḥy*). What
  is *waḥy*? A voice inaudible to sense-perception.[2]

The word "compulsion" (*jabr*) makes me impatient for
  Love's sake: 'tis only he that loves not that is fettered by
  compulsion.

This is communion with God, not compulsion: the shining
  of the moon, not a cloud:

Or, if it be compulsion, it is not ordinary compulsion: it is
  not the compulsion exerted by self-will, inciting us to
  sin.

O son, they alone know the true meaning of compulsion in
  whom God hath opened the heart's eye.[3]

---

[1] *Math.* I, 1456.

[2] Here and elsewhere Rūmī abolishes the orthodox distinction between the superior inspiration of prophets (*waḥy*) and the inferior of
saints (*ilhām*).

[3] "Compulsion" (*jabr*), as generally understood, implies conflict of
two wills and subjugation of the weaker. In this sense the term is anathema to Ṣūfīs who know and love God and, in selfless union (* maʿiyyah*)
with His Will, feel perfectly free. The blissful experience of living under
Divine Control may, however, be described technically as "laudable
compulsion" (*jabr-i maḥmūd*).

CII

⌣⌐ ⌣⌐ ⌣⌐ ⌣⌐ ⌣⌐ ⌣⌐ ⌣⌐ ⌣⌐ ⌣⌐

THE APOLOGY OF IBLĪS[1]

AT first I was an angel: with all my soul I trod the Way of devotion to the service of God.

How should one's first calling be forgotten? How should the first love fade away from one's heart?

Was it not the hand of His Bounty that saved me? Was it not He that raised me up from non-existence?

Who found milk for me in my infancy? Who rocked my cradle? He.

The nature that flows in with the milk—can it ever be expelled?

Bounty and Grace and Favour are the real substance of His coin, Wrath but a speck of alloy on it.

I regard not His Wrath, which is a temporary cause: I am regarding His eternally precedent Mercy.[2]

Grant that envy was the motive of my refusal to bow down before Adam; yet that envy arose from love of God, not from disobedience.

All envy arises from love, for fear lest another become the companion of the beloved.

----

[1] *Math.* II, 2617. On the theme of this passage, see Massignon, *La Passion d'al-Hallāj*, pp. 864–867 and *The Idea of Personality in Ṣūfism*, pp. 31–33. Iblīs depicts himself as the devoted lover whose jealousy forbids him to pay homage to a rival. In reality, he says, his refusal to glorify Adam was a declaration that he would worship none but God. He would suffer damnation rather than compromise the Divine Unity. Since his original nature was good, his disobedience can only be a transient lapse from grace.

[2] According to the Holy Tradition, "My Mercy preceded (or 'prevailed over') My Wrath."

Brooding jealousy is the inevitable consequence of love,
just as "Live Long!" must follow the sneeze.[3]

Since there was no move but this on His chessboard and He
bade me play, what else could I do?[4]

I played the one play that there was and cast myself into
woe.

Even in woe I taste His delights: I am mated by Him,
mated by Him, mated by Him!"[5]

---

[3] "Live long," *dīr zī*. Cf. Greek ζῆθι Latin *salve*. The usual Moslem
formulas are "God be praised!" (*al-ḥamd lillāh*) and "God have mercy
on you" (*yarḥamuk Allāh*).

[4] Iblīs, professing to know the mystery of predetermination (*sirru
'l-qadar*), pleads that it was impossible for him to obey a command which
God had eternally willed and decreed that he should disobey. Ḥallāj,
while applauding the "self-sacrifice" (*futuwwah*) of Iblīs, at the same
time insists on the duty of humble submission to the Divine Commandments.

[5] True lovers of God enjoy the pain their Beloved inflicts on them.

CIII

LOVE AND LOGIC[1]

LEARN from thy Father! He, not falsely proud,
With tears of sorrow all his sin avowed.[2]
Wilt thou, then, still pretend to be unfree
And clamber up Predestination's tree?—
Like Iblīs and his progeny abhorred,
In argument and battle with their Lord.
The blest initiates *know*: what need to *prove*?
From Satan logic, but from Adam love.

---

[1] *Math.* IV, 1389.
[2] After his fall from Paradise Adam repented and took the blame on himself (*Qur'ān* VII, 22). It is said that he alighted in Sarandīb (Ceylon) and shed floods of tears which caused every valley to be filled with fragrant plants and spices.

CIV

THE ONE TRUE LIGHT[1]

THE lamps are different, but the Light is the same: it comes from Beyond.

If thou keep looking at the lamp, thou art lost: for thence arises the appearance of number and plurality.

Fix thy gaze upon the Light, and thou art delivered from the dualism inherent in the finite body.

O thou who art the kernel of Existence, the disagreement between Moslem, Zoroastrian and Jew depends on the standpoint.

Some Hindus brought an elephant, which they exhibited in a dark shed.

As seeing it with the eye was impossible, every one felt it with the palm of his hand.

The hand of one fell on its trunk: he said, "This animal is like a water-pipe."

Another touched its ear: to him the creature seemed like a fan.

Another handled its leg and described the elephant as having the shape of a pillar.

Another stroked its back. "Truly," said he, "this elephant resembles a throne."

Had each of them held a lighted candle, there would have been no contradiction in their words.

---

[1] *Math.* III, 1259. Religions are many, God is One. The intellect, groping in the dark, cannot form any conception of His nature. Only the clairvoyant eye of the mystic sees Him as He really is.

‿‿‿‿‿‿‿‿‿‿‿

THE TWELVE GOSPELS[1]

THAT enemy of the religion of Jesus drew up twelve scriptures, each of which contradicted the other from beginning to end.

In one he made the path of asceticism and fasting to be the basis of repentance and the condition necessary for conversion.[2]

In one he said: "Asceticism profits naught: in this Way there is no salvation but through munificence."[3]

In one he said: "Both your abstinence and your muni-

---

[1] *Math.* I, 463. A fanatical Jewish King resolved to extirpate the Christians. Seeing that many secret adherents of the proscribed faith eluded his vengeance, he took counsel with his vizier, who suggested that the King should accuse him of being a Christian in disguise, mutilate him, and drive him into exile; then he would flee to the Christians, win their confidence, and compass their destruction. This plot was carried out. The vizier gradually brought the Christian community under his supreme rule. When all was ripe, he summoned twelve leaders chosen by himself and handed to each one a scroll, appointing him his successor, which was alleged to contain the true gospel of Christ, though in fact the contents of every scroll were different and irreconcilable. Then he killed himself, leaving the Christians to perish in the bitter fighting that immediately broke out among the twelve claimants to the succession.

Older Moslem versions of the legend identify the "vizier" with St. Paul, and it seems to reflect hostile criticism by Christian theologians who favoured St. Peter. Cf. the pseudo-Clementine "Apocalypse of Peter" (*Bulletin of the John Rylands Library* XV, No. 1, p. 179), where Paul is accused of tampering with the twelve books which contained the profession of faith of each of the twelve Apostles (p. 236).

[2] The doctrines mentioned here and below are Ṣūfistic, though in some cases their development was influenced by Christian theory and practice.

[3] "Munificence" (*jūd*), *i.e.* charity and generosity of soul as opposed to the externals of asceticism.

ficence imply that you associate regard for these objects with Him Who is the Object of your worship.[4]

Excepting trust in God and complete resignation in sorrow and joy, all is a deceit and a snare."

In one he said: "It behoves you to do service to God; the notion of putting trust in Him is suspicious."[5]

In one he said: "The Divine Commandments and Prohibitions are not meant for practice, but only to show our incapacity to fulfil them,

So that we may recognize our weakness and confess the power of the Almighty."[6]

In one he said: "Never mind your weakness: to dwell upon that is an act of ingratitude. Beware!

Regard your power and know that it was given you by Him who is the Absolute."[7]

In one he said, "Leave them both behind: whatsoever involves sense-perception is an idol."[8]

In one he said: "Do not put out this candle of sense-perception: it lights the way to interior concentration.[9]

If you discard sensation and phantasy too soon, you will have put out the lamp of union at midnight."

In one he said: "Put it out—have no fear—so that you may get perceptions thousandfold in exchange;

For by putting it out the light of the spirit is infinitely

---

[4] *i.e.* every form of self-activity and self-regard is "secret polytheism" (*shirk-i khafī*).

[5] If pushed to its extreme logical consequences, the doctrine of trust in God (*tawakkul*) would be incompatible with religious and social duties which no good Moslem can neglect.

[6] Alluding to the heresy of *jabr*. See Nos. XCVII–XCIX.

[7] See No. XCVII, note 1, and No. XCIX, note 5.

[8] "An idol," *i.e.* an obstacle to realization of the Divine Unity.

[9] The physical and mental faculties of Man enable him to fulfil the purpose for which he was created: without them he could never attain to perfect knowledge of God. Although they are of this world and cannot accompany him to his goal, yet before closing the eyes of sense and intellect he should make full use of such light as they can give to help him on the way.

increased: by your self-denial your Laylā (Beloved) becomes your Majnūn (lover)."

In one he said: "Seek a master to instruct you: among the qualities derived from ancestors you will not find foresight of the end."[10]

Every religious sect only foresaw the end as they themselves conceived it: consequently they fell captive to error.

To foresee the end is not as easy as hand-weaving; else how would there have been such differences of doctrine?

In one he said: "Be a man, be not a slave to men! Take your own course, do not run about in search of a master!"[11]

In one he said: "All this multiformity is one: whoever sees double is a squint-eyed manikin."

In one he said: "How can a hundred be one? He who thinks so is surely mad."

He had no comprehension of the purity of Jesus: he was not imbued with any tincture of the vat of Jesus,

From which the garment of a hundred dyes would emerge as simple and one-coloured as light.[12]

---

[10] "Foresight of the end" ('āqibat-bīnī), i.e. the mystical "second-sight" and universal gnosis reserved for those who have been initiated by a Ṣūfī Pīr. Others regard their own particular forms of belief as final.

[11] "Be a man," i.e. a holy man: prophets and saints are "the men" (mardān) par excellence. See No. XXVIII, note 3.

[12] Moslem authors relate that when Jesus, who was apprenticed to a dyer, cast many-coloured garments into the vat they came out white as snow. This is a parable of the heart of the Perfect Man, which purifies and unifies all that comes into touch with it.

⌐⌐⌐⌐⌐⌐⌐⌐⌐⌐⌐

THE SHEPHERD'S PRAYER[1]

MOSES saw a shepherd on the way, crying, "O Lord Who
  choosest as Thou wilt,

Where art Thou, that I may serve Thee and sew Thy
  shoon and comb Thy hair?

That I may wash Thy clothes and kill Thy lice and bring
  milk to Thee, O worshipful One;

That I may kiss Thy little hand and rub Thy little feet and
  sweep Thy little room at bed-time."

On hearing these foolish words, Moses said, "Man, to
  whom are you speaking?

What babble! What blasphemy and raving! Stuff some
  cotton into your mouth!

Truly the friendship of a fool is enmity: the High God is
  not in want of suchlike service."

The shepherd rent his garment, heaved a sigh, and took
  his way to the wilderness.

Then came to Moses a Revelation: "Thou hast parted My
  servant from Me.

Wert thou sent as a prophet to unite, or wert thou sent to
  sever?

I have bestowed on every one a particular mode of worship,
  I have given every one a peculiar form of expression.

The idiom of Hindustān is excellent for Hindūs; the idiom
  of Sind is excellent for the people of Sind.

I look not at tongue and speech, I look at the spirit and
  the inward feeling.

---

[1] *Math.* II, 1720.

I look into the heart to see whether it be lowly, though the words uttered be not lowly.

Enough of phrases and conceits and metaphors! I want burning, burning: become familiar with that burning!

Light up a fire of love in thy soul, burn all thought and expression away!

O Moses, they that know the conventions are of one sort, they whose souls burn are of another."

The religion of love is apart from all religions. The lovers of God have no religion but God alone.

CVII

⌐⌐⌐⌐⌐⌐⌐⌐⌐⌐⌐

A REBUKE TO BIGOTS[1]

On this wise did the Jew tell his dream. Oh, there is many
a Jew whose end was praiseworthy.[2]

Do not spurn any infidel, for it may be hoped that he will
die a Moslem.

What knowledge have you of the close of his life, that you
should once and for all avert your face from him?

---

[1] *Math.* VI, 2450.

[2] The Jew's "dream" refers to a mystical experience symbolized by
the epiphany (*tajallī*) of God in His Glory at Mt. Sinai. (*Qur'ān* VI, 139),
when "the mountain was shattered and Moses fell down in a swoon."

CVIII

RELIGIOUS CONTROVERSY[1]

THESE two-and-seventy sects will remain till the Resurrection: the heretic's talk and argument will not fail.[2]

The number of locks upon a treasure are the proof of its high value.

The long windings of the way, its mountain-passes, and the brigands infesting it, announce the greatness of the traveller's goal.

Every false doctrine resembles a mountain-pass, a precipice, and a brigand.

The blind religious are in a dilemma, for the champions on either side stand firm: each party is delighted with its own path.

Love alone can end their quarrel, Love alone comes to the rescue when you cry for help against their arguments.

Eloquence is dumbfounded by Love: it dare not engage in altercation.

The lover fears to answer back, lest the mystic pearl drop from his mouth.

'Tis as though a marvellous bird perched on your head, and your soul trembled for fear of its flitting:[3]

---

[1] *Math.* V, 3221.

[2] So long as this world lasts, the continuance of false beliefs is necessary and providential: they are formidable obstacles which serve to test the mettle of the "traveller" and must be overcome before he can win the "treasure" that is beyond price.

[3] When the Prophet recited the *Qur'ān*, his Companions (we are told) sat so still and listened so attentively that "one would think birds were perched on their heads." "The sparrow has flown from his head" is an Arabic proverb denoting fluster and perturbation.

You dare not move or breathe, you suppress a cough, lest
the phoenix should fly away;
And if any one speak, you lay a finger on your lip, meaning,
"Hush!"
Love is like that bird: it makes you silent: it puts the lid
on the boiling kettle.

CIX

THE DOCTRINE OF RESERVE[1]

WHEN news arrived of the face of Shamsu'ddīn, the sun in the Fourth Heaven hid itself for shame.[2]

Since his name has come to my life, it behoves me to give some hint of his bounty.

My soul plucks my skirt: she has caught the perfume of Joseph's vest.[3]

She said: "For the sake of our years of companionship, recount one of those sweet ecstasies,

That earth and heaven may laugh with joy, that intellect and spirit and eye may increase a hundredfold."

I said: "Do not lay tasks on me, for I have passed away from myself (*fanā*); my apprehensions are blunted, I know not how to praise.

'Tis unseemly, if one who has not yet returned to consciousness constrain himself to play the braggart.[4]

How should I—not a vein of mine is sensible—describe that Friend Who hath no peer?

The description of this desolate bleeding heart let me leave over till another time."

She answered: "Feed me, for I am hungry, and make haste, for the 'moment' (*waqt*) is a cutting sword.[5]

---

[1] *Math.* I, 123.

[2] "The face of Shamsu'ddīn," referring to Shams-i Tabrīz and metaphorically to the manifestation (*tajallī*) of God in the Perfect Man.

[3] "My soul," said by the commentators to signify Ḥusāmu'ddīn, with whom the poet feels himself mystically one. "The perfume of Joseph's vest," smelt from afar by Jacob (*Qur'ān* XII, 94), describes spiritual rapture.

[4] The Ṣūfī, when really "God-intoxicated," is unconscious of the boastful words that may fall from his lips.

[5] *Waqt*, a technical term for the "moment" of immediate mystical experience, is compared to a sharp sword, because "it cuts the root of the future and the past."

175

The Ṣūfī is the son of the 'moment' (*ibnu 'l-waqt*), O comrade: 'tis not the rule of the Way to say 'To-morrow.'[6]

Art not thou a Ṣūfī, then? That which is in hand is reduced to naught by postponing the payment."

I said to her: "Better that the secret of the Friend should be disguised: do thou hearken to it as implied in the contents of the tale.

Better that the lovers' secret should be told (allegorically) in the talk of others."[7]

She said: "Tell it forth openly and nakedly and without unfaithfulness: do not put me off, O trifler!

Lift the veil and speak nakedly. I do not wear a shirt when I sleep with the Adored One."

I said: "If He should become naked in thy vision, neither wilt thou endure nor thy bosom nor thy waist.

Ask thy wish, but ask with measure: a blade of straw cannot support a mountain.

If the Sun, by whom this world is illumined, approach a little nearer, all will be burned up.

Do not seek trouble and turmoil and bloodshed: say no more concerning the Sun of Tabrīz!"

---

[6] "The son of the moment" should live only in the present, whether he be an adept, whose "moment" is "the eternal Now," or a novice, who must learn that nothing good will come of him if he looks beyond his actual state and hopes to provide for the morrow.

[7] Even to the elect, the mysteries of gnosis can only be communicated—for "he who knows God is dumb"—through a screen of symbolism; and elsewhere Rūmī shows that he, like every Ṣūfī Shaykh, is well aware of the danger of any attempt to divulge them to outsiders.

CX

UNKNOWING[1]

Lo, for I to myself am unknown, now in God's name what must I do?

I adore not the Cross nor the Crescent, I am not a Giaour nor a Jew.

East nor West, land nor sea, is my home; I have kin nor with angel nor gnome;

I am wrought not of fire nor of foam, I am shaped not of dust nor of dew.

I was born not in China afar, not in Saqsīn and not in Bulghār;

Not in India, where five rivers are, nor 'Irāq nor Khorāsān I grew.

Not in this world nor that world I dwell, not in Paradise neither in Hell;

Not from Eden and Riẓwān I fell, not from Adam my lineage I drew.[2]

In a place beyond uttermost place, in a tract without shadow or trace,

Soul and body transcending I live in the Soul of my Loved One anew!

---

[1] *Dīwān, SP*, XXXI.
[2] Riẓwān, the Angel who keeps the keys of Paradise.

CXI

THE UNITIVE STATE[1]

I AM not a congener of the King—far be it from Him!—
but I have light from His radiance.[2]

Homogeneity is not in respect of form and essence: water
becomes homogeneous with earth in the plant.

Since my *genus* is not the *genus* of my King, my ego passed
away (*fanā*) for the sake of His Ego.

My ego passed away, He remains alone: I roll like dust
under His horse's feet.

The individual self became dust: the only trace of it is the
print of His feet upon its dust.[3]

Become dust at His feet for the sake of that footprint and
be as the diadem on the head of an Emperor!

---

[1] *Math.* II, 1170.

[2] Rūmī distinguishes (*Math.* V, 2038) "becoming one with the Light
of God" (*ittiḥād-i Nūr*) from "infusion" or "incarnation" (*ḥulūl*), which
involves homogeneity. God is Unique. The Perfect Man, though invested with all the Divine Attributes, is not God absolutely: he is real
(*ḥaqq*), but not *the* Real (*al-Ḥaqq*). So the Logos of Philo is θεός, but not
ὁΘεός (Bigg, *Christian Platonists of Alexandria*, 2nd ed., p. 42, note 2).

[3] The Perfect Man "bears the mark of God's feet on his dust," *i.e.* the
eternal imprint of the Divine Attributes which were stamped upon
him before he emerged from potentiality into actual existence; for "he
is to the universe what the bezel is to the seal—the bezel whereon is
graven the signature that the King seals on His treasuries" (Ibnu'l-
'Arabī, *Fuṣūṣ*, 13).

CXII

⌐_,⌐_,⌐_,⌐_,⌐_,⌐_,⌐_,⌐_,⌐_,⌐_,⌐_

THE LIFE EVERLASTING[1]

ALL human faculties are impermanent: they are naughted
on the Day of Resurrection;

Yet the light of the senses and spirits of our fathers is not
wholly perishable, like the grass.

Those who have passed from the world are not non-existent:
they are steeped in the Divine Attributes.

All their attributes are absorbed in the Attributes of God,
even as stars vanish in the presence of the sun.

If you demand authority from the *Qur'ān*, recite the text,
"All of them shall be brought into Our Presence (muḥḍarūn)."[2]

The person denoted by the word *muḥḍarūn* is not non-
existent. Meditate on this, so that you may gain certain
knowledge of the everlasting life of the spirit.

The spirit debarred from everlasting life in in torment; the
spirit everlastingly united with God is free from barriers.

---

[1] *Math.* IV, 431.
[2] *Qur'ān* XXXVI, 32 and 53. At the Resurrection all mankind shall
be assembled in the presence of God. Rūmī, of course, applies this text
to the mystical death (*fanā*) which is life without end (*baqā*).

CXIII

⌣⌣⌣⌣⌣⌣⌣⌣⌣⌣

DOES PERSONALITY SURVIVE?[1]

THERE is no dervish in the world; and if there be, that
dervish is really non-existent.[2]

He exists in respect of the survival of his essence, but his
attributes are extinguished in the Attributes of God.[3]

Like the flame of a candle in the presence of the sun, he is
really non-existent, though he exists in formal calcula-
tion.

The flame's essence is existent in so far as if you put cotton
upon it, the cotton will be consumed;

But in reality it is non-existent: it gives you no light, the
sun has naughted it.

When an ounce of vinegar is dissolved in a hundred maunds
of sugar

---

[1] *Math.* III, 3669. The term *fanā* is used by Ṣūfīs in connexion with
different theories as to the nature of mystical union and may imply:

(1) that the *essence* of the creature (*dhāt-i ʿabd*) passes away (*fānī
shavad*) in the Essence of God and ceases to exist, just as a drop of water
loses its individuality (*taʿayyun*) in the ocean;

(2) that the *attributes* of the creature (*ṣifāt-i ʿabd*) pass away in the
Attributes of God: his human attributes are changed (*mubaddal*) into
Divine Attributes, so that God becomes his ear and eye;

(3) that the *essence* of the creature vanishes in the Light of the Divine
Essence, like the disappearance of stars in the light of the sun. His
creatureliness (*khalqiyyah*) does not cease to exist, but is concealed
(*makhfī*) under the aspect of Creativeness (*Ḥaqqiyyah*): the Lord (*Rabb*)
is manifest, the slave (*ʿabd*) invisible.

[2] Here "dervish" stands for the perfect type of spiritual poverty, the
saint who is denuded of self and dead to the world, even if he appears
to live in it.

[3] Nominally he exists, for his "person" (*dhāt-i bashariyyah*) is not
annihilated; but since it has been transfigured and "deified," he is
really non-existent as an individual and only survives (*bāqī hast*) in
virtue of the Divine Life and Energy which constitute his whole being.

The acid flavour is non-existent when you taste the sugar, albeit the ounce exists as a surplus when you weigh.

In the presence of a lion the deer becomes senseless: her existence is but a veil for his.

Analogies drawn by imperfect men concerning the action of the Lord are like the emotion of love, they are not irreverent.

The lover's pulse bounds up unabashed, he levels himself with the King.

He appears irreverent, for his claim of love involves equality with the Beloved;

But look deeper: what does he claim? Both he and his claim are naughted in the presence of that Sultan.

Māta Zayd^{un} (Zayd died): if Zayd is the agent (grammatical subject), yet he is not the agent, since he is defunct.

He is the agent only in respect of the grammatical expression; otherwise he is the one acted upon, and Death is his slayer.

What ability to act remains in one who has been so overpowered that all the qualities of an agent are gone from him?

⌣‚⌣‚⌣‚⌣‚⌣‚⌣‚⌣‚⌣‚⌣‚⌣

THE SOUL OF THE WORLD[1]

I HAVE circled awhile with the nine Fathers in each
    Heaven.[2]

For years I have revolved with the stars in their signs.

I was invisible awhile, I was dwelling with Him.

I was in the Kingdom of "*or nearer*," I saw what I have
    seen.[3]

I receive my nourishment from God, as a child in the
    womb;

Man is born once, I have been born many times.[4]

Clothed in a bodily mantle, I have busied myself with
    affairs,

And often have I rent the mantle with my own hands.

I have passed nights with ascetics in the monastery,

I have slept with infidels before the idols in the pagoda.

I am the pangs of the jealous, I am the pain of the sick.

---

[1] *Dīwān, SP*, 331. A description of the Perfect Man as the Universal
Spirit.

[2] "The nine Fathers": each of the nine celestial spheres was supposed
to have a ruling Intelligence, and these spiritual powers are called
"Fathers" here. "The *seven* Fathers" is a phrase commonly applied to
the planets; some raise the number to nine by adding the Head and Tail
of the "Dragon" of astrology (note on *Math.* I, 3991), but such an
explanation is hardly satisfying.

[3] Cf. *Qur'ān* LIII, 8–10: "then he approached and descended and
was at a distance of two bow-lengths or nearer"—a passage which is
generally interpreted as the climax of the Prophet's ascension.

[4] "Man is born once," a hard saying for some modern writers who
foist upon Rūmī the Indian doctrine of re-birth. Only the mystic "is
born many times," and his experience of birth, death and resurrection
belongs to quite a different order of ideas: in reality it typifies the movement of the World-Spirit, with which he is one, evolving through lower
forms of soul-life and manifesting itself finally and completely in the
Perfect Man. Cf. Nos. LXXXVIII and CXVIII.

I am both cloud and rain: I have rained on the meadows.
Never did the dust of mortality settle on my skirt, O
dervish!
I have gathered a wealth of roses in the garden of Eternity.
I am not of water nor fire, I am not of the froward wind,
I am not of moulded clay: I have mocked at them all.
O son, I am not Shams-i Tabrīz, I am the pure Light.
If thou seest me, beware! Tell not any one what thou hast
seen!

CXV

⌣⌣⌣⌣⌣⌣⌣⌣⌣⌣

DEIFICATION[1]

WHEN a fly is plunged in honey, all the members of its body are reduced to the same condition, and it does not move. Similarly the term *istighrāq* (absorption in God) is applied to one who has no conscious existence or initiative or movement. Any action that proceeds from him is not his own. If he is still struggling in the water, or if he cries out, "Oh, I am drowning," he is not said to be in the state of absorption. This is what is signified by the words *Ana 'l-Ḥaqq* "I am God." People imagine that it is a presumptuous claim, whereas it is really a presumptuous claim to say *Ana 'l-ʿabd* "I am the slave of God"; and *Ana 'l-Ḥaqq* "I am God" is an expression of great humility. The man who says *Ana 'l-ʿabd* "I am the slave of God" affirms two existences, his own and God's, but he that says *Ana 'l-Ḥaqq* "I am God" has made himself non-existent and has given himself up and says "I am God," *i.e.* "I am naught, He is all: there is no being but God's." This is the extreme of humility and self-abasement.

---

[1] *Fīhi mā fīhi*, 49. See No. LXXXVIII, note 5, and cf. *Math.* II, 1346: When he (the mystic) falls into the dyeing-vat of *Hū* (the Absolute God), and you say to him, "Arise," he cries in rapture, "I am the vat: do not blame me." That "I am the vat" is the same as saying "I am God" (*ana 'l-Ḥaqq*): he has the colour of fire, albeit he is iron.

The colour of the iron is naughted in the colour of the fire: the iron boasts of its fierceness, though actually it is silent.
It has become glorified by the colour and nature of the fire: it says, "I am the fire, I am the fire."

CXVI

THE GOD-MAN[1]

To praise and glorify him is to glorify God: Divine fruit is
  growing from the essential nature of this tray.
Apples grow from this basket in fine variety: 'tis no harm
  if you bestow on it the name of "tree."
Call this basket "the Apple-tree," for between the two
  there is a secret union.
Deem this basket to be the Tree of Fortune and sit happily
  beneath its shade.

---

[1] *Math.* VI, 3204. In this analogy "the Apple-tree" is God, and the
Perfect Man is likened to a tray or basket of apples, *i.e.* Divine Attributes,
which provide spiritual food for all who believe in him.

CXVII

THE SPIRITUAL ASCENSION[1]

IF you join the ranks of those who make the Ascension,
    not-being will bear you aloft like Burāq.[2]
'Tis not like the ascension of a mortal to the moon; nay,
    but like the ascension of a sugar-cane to sugar.
'Tis not like the ascension of a vapour to the sky; nay, but
    like the ascension of an embryo to rationality.

---

[1] *Math.* IV, 552.
[2] "Not-being," *i.e.* the passing away (*fanā*) of self-consciousness.
Burāq is the steed on which the Prophet is said to have ridden to Heaven.

CXVIII

THE PROGRESS OF MAN[1]

FIRST he appeared in the realm inanimate;
Thence came into the world of plants and lived
The plant-life many a year, nor called to mind
What he had been; then took the onward way
To animal existence, and once more
Remembers naught of that life vegetive.
Save when he feels himself moved with desire
Towards it in the season of sweet flowers,
As babes that seek the breast and know not why.[2]

---

[1] *Math.* IV, 3637. The doctrine of soul-development set forth by Rūmī in this and other passages, *e.g.* Nos. V (note 2), XLII (note 3), LXI and LXV, is not peculiar to him: it appears in Moslem philosophy and mysticism at a much earlier date and is founded on Aristotle's theory of the triple nature of the soul as poetically described by Milton (*Paradise Lost* V, 479 *seqq.*):

> So from the root
> Springs lighter the green stalk, from thence the leaves
> More aery, last the bright consummate flower
> Spirits odorous breathes: flowers and their fruit,
> Man's nourishment, by gradual scale sublimed,
> To vital spirits aspire, to animal,
> To intellectual; give both life and sense,
> Fancy and understanding; whence the Soul
> Reason receives, and Reason is her being.

To complete the parallel, these lines should be read in connexion with Milton's treatise *De doctrinâ Christianâ*, where he elaborates the view that "all creation, inanimate and animate, consists but of diverse forms or degrees of one and the same original or prime *matter*; which *matter* was originally an efflux or emanation out of the very substance of the One Eternal Spirit" (Masson, *The Poetical Works of John Milton*, III, 361).

[2] The functions of the vegetive soul are growth, assimilation, and reproduction. Spring flowers and verdure awaken in the animal soul, which is the "child" of the vegetive soul, subconscious memories of its "mother."

Again the wise Creator whom thou knowest
Uplifted him from animality
To Man's estate; and so from realm to realm
Advancing, he became intelligent,
Cunning and keen of wit, as he is now.
No memory of his past abides with him,
And from his present soul he shall be changed.

Though he is fallen asleep, God will not leave him
In this forgetfulness. Awakened, he
Will laugh to think what troublous dreams he had,
And wonder how his happy state of being
He could forget and not perceive that all
Those pains and sorrows were the effect of sleep
And guile and vain illusion. So this world
Seems lasting, though 'tis but the sleeper's dream;
Who, when the appointed Day shall dawn, escapes
From dark imaginings that haunted him,
And turns with laughter on his phantom griefs
When he beholds his everlasting home.

CXIX

"RIPENESS IS ALL"[1]

Since thou canst not bear the unveiled Light, drink the
Word of Wisdom, for its light is veiled,[2]

To the end that thou mayst become able to receive the
Light, and behold without veils that which now is
hidden,

And traverse the sky like a star; nay, journey unconditioned, without a sky.

'Twas thus thou camest into being from non-existence.
How didst thou come? Thou camest insensibly.[3]

The ways of thy coming thou rememberest not, but I will
give thee an indication.

Let thy mind go, then be mindful! Close thine ear, then
listen!

Nay, I will not tell, for thou art still unripe: thou art in
thy springtime, thou hast not seen the summer.

This world is as the tree: we are like the half-ripened fruit
upon it.

The unripe fruits cling fast to the bough, because they are
not fit for the palace;

But when they have ripened and become sweet and delicious—after that, they lose hold of the bough.

Even so does the kingdom of the world lose its savour for

---

[1] *Math.* III, 1286.

[2] By devoting himself to his Shaykh and absorbing spiritual truth in
the form of words the disciple is gradually prepared for entrance, if God
will, into the illuminative and contemplative life.

[3] "From non-existence," *i.e.* from the unobjectified world of Unity.
See No. LXIV and No. V.

him whose mouth has been sweetened by the great felicity.

Something remains untold, but the Holy Spirit will tell thee without me as the medium.

Nay, thou wilt tell it to thine own ear—neither I nor another, O thou who art one with me—

Just as, when thou fallest asleep, thou goest from the presence of thyself into the presence of thyself

And hearest from thyself that which thou thinkest is told thee secretly by some one in the dream.4

O good friend, thou art not a single "thou": thou art the sky and the deep sea.

Thy mighty infinite "Thou" is the ocean wherein myriads of "thou's" are sunken.

Do not speak, so that thou mayst hear from the Speakers what cannot be uttered or described.

Do not speak, so that the Spirit may speak for thee: in the ark of Noah leave off swimming!

---

4 The mysteries revealed in veridical dreams are not really communicated to the dreamer by the apparitions with which he imagines he is conversing. Nothing is external to the soul that knows God to be its true self and sees its descent and ascent as phases of His timeless Self-revelation.

TALES OF MYSTIC MEANING

*Selections from the Mathnawí of
Jalál-ud-Dín Rúmí*

CONTENTS

CONTENTS

CONTENTS

INTRODUCTION

I

THE conquest of Persia by the Arabs produced, among other things, an Islamic literature in the Persian language, very different in character from the contemporary Arabic literature (though of course they have much in common), and expressing unmistakably the genius of the gifted race which *capta ferum victorem cepit*. Of this literature the best part, in every meaning of the phrase, was composed by poets; and for a thousand years Persian poetry has been the chief interpreter of Persian thought to other peoples, both in the East and the West. Its first triumphs were won in the fields of epic and romance. If Firdawsī may not be compared with Homer, the *Shāhnāma* nevertheless is a worthy monument to the Heroic Age of Iran, from Jamshīd, who "gloried and drank deep," and Rustam, the unwitting slayer of his own son, through Darius and Alexander the Great down to the rise of the Sāsānian Empire with Ardashīr Bābakān and

its fall in the reign of Yazdigird. While this great
national poem finds admirers in many nations,
the romantic masterpieces of Nizāmī are dis-
appointing when translated; the style is too
subtle and obscure, the treatment of the subject
too conventional, to appeal strongly to us.
Meanwhile the art of panegyric had culminated
in Anwarī, and the quatrain or *rubāʿī* had established itself as the vehicle for epigrammatic—in
the Greek sense—criticism of life. The collection attributed to Omar Khayyām resembles the
Greek Anthology in being the work of various
more or less eminent hands, known and unknown, early and late. The extent of Omar's
share in it is uncertain. Very few of the *rubāʿiyāt*
can be definitely assigned to him, and a great
number of them cannot possibly be his; but,
taken together, they present characteristic ideas
with such simplicity and elegance that we may
excuse Fitzgerald for having made their reputed
author by far the most famous and popular of all
Persian writers in the Western literary world.
Besides epic, romance, panegyric, and epigram,
there was another type of poetry—the mystical
and ethical—which had been gaining ground
from the eleventh century onwards, and, after

the Mongol Invasion, not only eclipsed its rivals but attained an almost absolute supremacy in its own kind. Drawing inspiration from the religious philosophy of the Sūfīs, it seeks to shadow forth, in beautiful symbolic imagery, the emanation of all things from God and their ultimate re-union with Him, the longing of the mystic lover for the Beloved, his inward purification and transformation through suffering, his ecstasies and despairs—and, when the last veil has fallen away, his seeing "with the eye of certainty" that there is no "other" and that the Truth is essentially One. We need not discuss here the spiritual love-lyrics and wine-songs which were often chanted, with or without an accompaniment of music, in order to rouse emotion and induce ecstasy, and in some cases were composed with that object. Many Sūfīs were teachers as well as enthusiasts. In their didactic works the transcendental aspects of the doctrine may occupy an unimportant place or, at least, be combined with "a loftily inculcated ethical system, which recognises in charity, purity of heart, self-renunciation, and bridling of the passions the necessary conditions of eternal happiness." Among *mathnawīs* (poems in rhymed couplets) of this class the *Hadīqatu 'l-Haqīqat*, or "Garden of Truth," by Sanā'ī of Ghazna and the *Mantiqu 't-Tayr* or "Bird-Speech" by 'Attār of Nīshāpūr deserve mention on their merits, and also because Jalālu'ddīn Rūmī, the author of "The Mathnawī" *par excellence*, regarded Sanā'ī and 'Attār as his masters in Sūfism.

II

Born at Balkh in 1207, Jalālu'ddīn belonged
to a family claiming descent from the Caliph
Abū Bakr and allied with the royal house of
Khwārazm (Khiva), his grandfather having
married a daughter of Sultān Muhammad
Khwārazmshāh. In 1206 this monarch annexed
Balkh to his empire. At that time he was a
zealous Sunnī, and he is so described in one of
the stories in the *Mathnawī* (see p. 128 *infra*);
but soon afterwards he embraced the Shī'ite
heresy, a step that must have been bitterly re-
sented by the orthodox citizens of Balkh, in-
cluding the poet's father, Bahā'u'ddīn Walad,
a man distinguished for piety and learning. We
are told that Bahā'u'ddīn incurred the wrath
of Khwārazmshāh and left the city, accompanied
by his family, when Jalālu'ddīn was still a child.
After long wanderings, in the course of which
they visited Baghdād, Mecca, and Damascus,
the exiles arrived in Rūm (Asia Minor), and
finally settled at Qōniya (Iconium) under the
protection of the Seljūq Sultān 'Alā'u'ddīn
Kayqubād. Here Jalālu'ddīn spent the last fifty

years of his life, whence he is known as "Rūmī."
He died in 1273, leaving two sons and a
daughter.

If one can scarcely think of Plato without
Socrates, still less is it possible to separate
Jalālu'ddīn Rūmī from Shams-i Tabrīz, the
mysterious dervish under whose name he published his *Dīwān* and with whom he identified
himself so intimately that the very existence of
his *alter ego* has been doubted, in my opinion
unwarrantably. The history of Sūfism affords
many examples of enthusiastic friendship between teachers and disciples, and the *Mathnawī*
shows that after the death of Shams-i Tabrīz
the poet stood in a similar mystic relation to
Husāmu'ddīn Chelebi, who succeeded him as
Head of the Mevlevī Order of Dervishes—the
Order founded by Jalālu'ddīn in memory, it is
said, of Shams-i Tabrīz, with "their tall drab-
coloured felt hats and wide cloaks," their reed-
flutes and rebecks, and their whirling dance.
It was a wild flock that he and the inner group
of saintly men who gathered round him at
Qōniya were called upon to shepherd. Such a
task demanded immense energy, experience,
and knowledge of the world. That he composed

most of his poetry while engaged in organising and directing the affairs of a great Brotherhood would be incredible if we did not know, from St. Paul, for instance, what strength is given by the union of deep mystical faith with an intense and creative personality.

III

The *Mathnawī*, frequently described as the *Qur'ān-i Pahlawī* or *Qur'ān* of Persia, belongs to the last period of his life, and was begun at the request of his favourite disciple, Husā-mu'ddīn Chelebi, who acted as amanuensis. Its six Books were composed at intervals during approximately fifteen years, and in the oldest manuscripts amount to rather less than 26,000 verses; in the Persian and Indian editions this total is greatly increased by interpolations. The author died before finishing the Sixth Book. The so-called Seventh Book was added in the seventeenth century by Ismā'īl Anqiravī, who wrote a Turkish commentary on the poem. Books I and II have been translated by Sir James Redhouse[1] and Dr. C. E. Wilson[2] respectively, and a complete version by the present writer is in course of publication.[3] The contents

[1] *The Mesnevī of Mevlānā Jelālu'd-dīn Muhammed er-Rūmī. Book the First. . . . Translated and the poetry versified by James W. Redhouse.* (*London*, 1881.)

[2] *The Masnavī by Jalālu'd-dīn Rūmī. Book II translated for the first time from the Persian into prose, with a Commentary,* by C. E. Wilson. (*London*, 1910.)

[3] *The Mathnawī of Jalālu'ddīn Rūmī. Edited from the*

of the work are excellently summarised by
E. H. Whinfield.[1] With all its faults—and from
a modern point of view they are many—the
Mathnawī exhibits, more fully than the *Dīwān-i
Shams-i Tabrīz*, the marvellous range of Jalālu'ddīn's poetical genius. His *Odes* reach the
utmost heights of which a poetry inspired by
vision and rapture is capable, and these alone
would have made him the unchallenged laureate
of Mysticism. But they move in a world remote
from ordinary experience, open to none but
"the unveiled," whereas the *Mathnawī* is chiefly
concerned with problems and speculations
bearing on the conduct, use, and meaning of
Life. While the *Odes* depict Reality as reflected
in the clairvoyant consciousness of the Saint,
the *Mathnawī* represents the Saint not only as a
mirror of Reality, but also as a personage invested
with Divine authority and power, an indispensable Guide on the Way to God, a Physician
who can diagnose and cure diseases of the

*oldest manuscripts available, with critical notes, translation
and commentary, by R. A. Nicholson. E. J. W. Gibb Memorial
Fund, New Series, IV. (London and Leiden, 1925—.)*

[1] *Masnavī-i Ma'navī, the Spiritual Couplets of Manlānā
Jalālu'd-dīn Muhammed Rūmī, translated and abridged by
E. H. Whinfield. (London, 1887; 2nd ed., 1898.)*

soul, a Preacher of the Truth and a Teacher of the Law—the law of reverent obedience, through which "Heaven was filled with light and the Angels became pure and holy." Professing to expound the esoteric doctrine of the *Qur'ān*, this vast rambling discourse provides instruction and entertainment for all seekers. Few would care to read it through; but everyone can find in it something to suit his taste, from abstruse and recondite theories of mystical philosophy to anecdotes of a certain kind, which are told in the plainest terms possible. Although the work as a whole lacks any comprehensive plan, the subjects treated in each Book are logically connected; so many digressions, however, intervene that the most attentive reader will often lose the thread of the argument. This is not the place to consider the author's ideas in detail. He may be called a Pantheist, with the reservation that at times he uses language inconsistent with Pantheism and implying belief in a personal God: he seems to have held the one and the other view as higher and lower aspects of the same Truth. The full pantheistic doctrine is for the spiritually perfect, not for the self-indulgent who draw immoral inferences

from it. So far as the "swine" are concerned,
Jalālu'ddīn, instead of casting his pearls before
them, recognises evil and sin as positive facts
and asserts that men are the *willing* slaves of
passion and therefore responsible for the wickedness they commit. They suffer tribulation and
punishment inflicted by Divine justice; yet as
His Mercy preceded His Wrath in the beginning, so shall it prevail in the end. The moral and
mystical teaching of the *Mathnawī* is centred
in Love. If even an earthly love can purify the
soul, how much greater must be the power of
the Love that leaves "nothing of myself in me"!
By developing this principle the poet shows
that all partial evil is universal good; that the
antithesis of freedom and necessity disappears
in harmony of will; and that a religious faith
resting on conventional beliefs or intellectual
evidences has no value whatever.

Allegory, the hard-worked handmaid of
Mysticism, can claim Sūfī literature as her
capital province, in which all her features—
sublime, exquisite, fantastic, and grotesque—
are represented on the most imposing scale.
Though much of the symbolism may be found
elsewhere, a great deal is peculiar and unique,

so that the writings in which it occurs seldom impart their real significance except to those who possess the key to the cipher, while the uninitiated will either understand them literally or not at all. But allegory may also be employed, in the form of fables, anecdotes, apologues, and parables, for the purpose of exposition and illustration; and here it serves, not as a mask or secret code, but as a means of teaching moral and mystical truths by leading the disciple through the familiar to the strange, through the seen to the unseen, through the letter to the spirit.

IV

Following, or rather adapting to his own needs, a method long established in Sūfī poetry, Jalālu'ddīn sets the matter of his discourse within a framework of Tales, which introduce and exemplify the various topics and are frequently interwoven with explanations of their inner meaning. These explanations in their turn may suggest other Tales, which demand fresh explanations, and so it goes on till the original Tale is concluded, when the same process begins over again. The *Mathnawī* is a grand Storybook. There are several hundreds of stories, comprising specimens in almost every *genre*, and no one can accuse the author of lacking invention or fail to admire the easy power with which he moulds his raw material into whatever shape he will. As might be expected, the largest class consists of legends from the *Qur'ān* and its Commentaries, the Traditions of the Prophet, and the Lives of pre-Mohammedan prophets and Muslim saints. *Kalīla and Dimna*, the Arabic version of the Sanskrit *Pancha-tantra*, supplies numerous Beast Fables, where the animals play the allegorical parts assigned to them. Jalālu'ddīn borrows much but owes little: he makes his own everything that comes to hand. The First Story in the poem is taken from Ibn Sīnā (Avicenna); others can be traced back to Sanā'ī, Nizāmī, and 'Attār; and probably a large number were contributed by popular collections of anecdotes like the *Jawāmiʿu l-Hikāyāt* of 'Awfī. What precisely these literary sources were, and how far they cover the whole ground, is a question that has yet to be investigated. It is likely, I think, that some, perhaps many, of the Tales belong to the miscellaneous stock of "wandering" stories carried to and fro by dervishes and other travellers, in which case the author may have put them into verse from memory.

The Tales themselves, as distinguished from the doctrinal exegesis with its accompanying reflections, exhortations, and arguments, occupy a comparatively small space. Nor will the reader find in them what often makes the *Mathnawī* supreme poetry—lofty and sustained flights of imagination, or passages in which the fervour of the poet's eloquence and the fullness and rapidity of his thought remind one of a fire leaping forward and kindling itself by the impetus of its flames. But such qualities are not in keeping with narrative, and the Tales have their proper merits. Their direct semi-colloquial style, rising to dignity where the subject requires it, contrasts favourably with the artificial diction of most Persian verse. They abound in lively dialogue, masterly satiric and humorous descriptions of human nature, pictures of life and manners illustrating the outlook not only of medieval Sūfism but of Muslims generally, and lessons of universal application drawn from a wisdom that never plays on the surface without contemplating the hidden depths below. Great poet as he is, Jalālu'ddīn loves Truth more than Art. In his *Odes* the tide of enthusiasm sweeps all moralities before it, in the *Mathnawī* he rubs them in with a persistence which renders selection and abridgment necessary. "Listen to this Story," he says, "for 'tis the very marrow of thy inward state"—*mutato nomine de te fabula narratur;* but, unlike Horace, he does not know when to stop. Even his *jocularia*, some of which are far from edifying, turn themselves into ethical homilies or philosophical discourses. Still, the Tales are worth reading, husk, kernel and all. One feels that the Master enjoyed making them and that his disciples (whom he occasionally rebukes for being impatient to hear the rest of the story) must have enjoyed them too.

V

The following fifty-one Stories are a fair sample of the *Mathnawī* on the side from which the best general view of its spirit and character can be obtained by readers approaching it for the first time. All these versions except two are in prose, and are based upon the text and literal translation already published in the E. J. W. Gibb Memorial Series as far as the end of the Fourth Book; they also include a few short anecdotes from Book V. The force and savour of the *Mathnawī* would be lost in a paraphrase, and though I have modified here and there my complete translation, which is intended for students, the changes hardly affect its closeness to the original. I have tried to present the Tales attractively as well as faithfully. Their variety and interest become more apparent when they are arranged without regard to their position and sequence in the Six Books. Many, especially the longer ones, need pruning and trimming; and I decided to lighten them rather than leave them out altogether. As a rule, the temptation to give extracts has been resisted. No one likes unfinished stories; if the Poet sometimes breaks off in the middle, it is because his audience knew the end. Brief notes have been added, supplementing his own remarks on the allegorical sense and explaining allusions to matters with which only Muslims are usually familiar. A curious and interesting commentary might be written on the Tales. There is no room for it here, and in any case it could not commend them to the reader half so well as has been done by letting them speak for themselves.

R. A. N.

I

THE KING AND THE HANDMAIDEN[1]

IN olden time there was a King to whom belonged
the power temporal and also the power spiritual.

It chanced that one day he rode with his cour-
tiers to the chase.

On the king's highway the King espied a
Handmaiden: the soul of the King was en-
thralled by her.

Forasmuch as the bird, his soul, was fluttering
in its cage, he gave money and bought the
Handmaiden.

After he had bought her and won to his desire,
by Divine destiny she sickened.

The King gathered the physicians together
from left and right and said to them, "The
life of us both is in your hands.

My life is of no account, but she is the life of
my life. I am in pain and wounded: she is my
remedy.

[1] Book I, *v.* 36 foll. The allegory is plain enough. The
King typifies the rational spirit; the Handmaiden in love
with the Goldsmith is the soul enamoured of worldly
pleasure; the Physician, who by poisoning the Goldsmith
cures the Handmaiden of her passion, is the divinely inspired Saint.

Whoever heals her that is my life will bear away with him my treasure and pearls, large and small."

They all answered him, saying, "We will hazard our lives and summon all our skill and put it into the common stock.

Each one of us is the Messiah of a multitude:[1] in our hands is a medicine for every pain."

In their arrogance they did not say, "If God will"; therefore God showed unto them the weakness of Man.

The more cures and remedies they applied, the more did the illness increase, and their need was not fulfilled.

The sick girl became thin as a hair, while the eyes of the King flowed with tears of blood, like a river.

How it became manifest to the King that the physicians were unable to cure the Handmaiden, and how he turned his face towards God and dreamed of a holy man.

When the King saw the powerlessness of those physicians, he ran bare-footed to the mosque.

[1] Or, according to the oldest MS., "each one of us is a learned Messiah." The *Masīh*, of course, is Jesus, who says in the *Qur'ān*, iii, 43, "*I will heal the blind from birth and the leper, and I will bring the dead to life by permission of Allah.*"

He entered the mosque and advanced to the *mihrāb*[1] to pray: the prayer-carpet was bathed in the King's tears.

On coming to himself out of the flood of ecstasy he opened his lips in goodly praise and laud,

Saying, "O Thou whose least gift is the empire of the world, what shall I say? for Thou knowest the hidden thing.

O Thou with whom we always take refuge in our need, once again we have lost the way;

But Thou hast said, 'Albeit I know thy secret, nevertheless declare it in thine outward act.' "

When from the depths of his soul he raised a cry of supplication, the sea of Bounty began to surge.

Slumber overtook him in the midst of weeping: he dreamed that an old man appeared

And said, "Good tidings, O King! Thy prayers are granted. If to-morrow a stranger come to thee, he is from me.

He is the skilled physician: deem him veracious, for he is trusty and true.

In his remedy behold absolute magic, in his nature behold the might of God!"

---

[1] The niche indicating the direction of Mecca.

*The meeting of the King with the divine Physician
whose coming had been announced to him in a
dream.*

When the promised hour arrived and day broke
and the sun, rising from the east, began to
burn the stars,

The King was in the belvedere, expecting to see
that which had been shown mysteriously.

He saw a person excellent and worshipful, a
sun amidst a shadow,

Coming from afar, like the new moon in slender-
ness and radiance: he was non-existent,[1]
though existent in the form of phantasy.

In the stranger's countenance the King discerned the phantom which he had beheld in
his dream.

He himself, instead of the chamberlains, went
forward to meet his guest from the Invisible.

Both were seamen who had learned to swim, the
souls of both were knit together without
sewing.

The King said, "Thou wert my Beloved in
reality, not she; but in this world one action
arises from another.

O thou who art to me as Mustafā,[2] while I

---

[1] *i.e.* in the material world.
[2] Mohammed.

4

am like unto 'Umar[1]—I will gird my loins to
do thee service."

The King opened his hands and clasped him to
his breast and received him, like love, into
his heart and soul,

And kissed his hand and brow and inquired
concerning his home and journey.

So with many a question he led him to the place
of honour. "At last," he said, "I have found
a treasure by being patient.

O gift from God and defence against trouble,
O thou who art the meaning of 'Patience
is the key to joy,'

O thou whose countenance is the answer to
every question, by thee hard knots are loosed
without discussion.

Thou readest all that is in our hearts, thou
givest a helping hand to everyone whose foot
is in the mire."

*How the King led the Physician to the bedside of
the sick girl, that he might see her condition.*

When that meeting and bounteous spiritual
repast was over, he took his hand and conducted him to the harem.

He rehearsed the tale of the invalid and her
sickness and then seated him beside her.

The Physician observed the colour of her

[1] The second Caliph.

5

face and felt her pulse; he heard both the symptoms and the circumstances of her malady.

He said, "None of the remedies which they have applied builds up health; those false physicians have wrought destruction.

They were ignorant of the inward state. I seek refuge with God from that which they devise."

He saw the pain, and the secret became open to him, but he concealed it and did not tell the King.

Her pain was not caused by black or yellow bile: the smell of every firewood appears from the smoke.

From her sore grief he perceived that she was heart-sore; well in body but stricken in heart.

Being in love is made manifest by soreness of heart: there is no sickness like heart-sickness.

The lover's ailment is separate from all other ailments: Love is the astrolabe of divine mysteries.

Whether Love be from this side or from that,[1] in the end it leads us Yonder.

How the Physician demanded of the King to be alone with the Handmaiden for the purpose of discovering her malady.

He said, "O King, make the house empty; send away both kinsfolk and strangers.

[1] *i.e.* earthly or heavenly.

6

Let no one listen in the entrance-halls, that I
may ask certain things of this handmaiden."

The house was left empty, not one inhabitant
remained, nobody save the Physician and the
sick girl.

Very gently he asked, "Where is thy native
town? for the treatment suitable to the people
of each town is different.

And in that town who is related to thee? With
whom hast thou kinship and affinity?"

She disclosed to the Physician many things
touching her home and former masters and
fellow-townsmen,

And he, while listening to her story, continued
to observe her pulse and its beating,

So that, if it throbbed at anyone's name, he
might know who was the object of her desire
in the world.

She told of many a town and many a house, and
still no vein of her quivered nor did her cheek
grow pale.

Her pulse kept its wonted time, unimpaired,
till he asked about sweet Samarcand.

Then it jumped, and her face went red and
pale by turns, for she had been parted from
a man of Samarcand, a Goldsmith.

When the Physician found out this secret from
the sick girl, he perceived the source of that
grief and woe.

7

He asked, "In which quarter of the town does he dwell?"

"*Sar-i Pul* (Bridge-head)," she replied, "and *Ghātafar* Street."

"I know," said he, "what your illness is, and I will at once display the arts of magic in delivering you.

Be glad and care-free and have no fear, for I will do to you that which rain does to the meadow.

I will be anxious for you, be not you anxious: I am kinder to you than a hundred fathers.

Beware! tell not this secret to anyone, not though the King himself should make much inquiry.

Let your heart become the grave of your secret, the sooner will your desire be gained.

When seeds are hidden in the earth, their inward secret becomes the verdure of the garden."

How the King sent messengers to Samarcand to fetch the Goldsmith.

Then he arose and went to the King and acquainted him with a part of the matter.

"The best plan," said he, "is that we should bring the man here for the purpose of curing this malady.

Summon the Goldsmith from that far coun-

8

try; beguile him with gold and robes of
honour."

The King sent thither two messengers, clever
men and competent and very just.

To Samarcand came the two messengers for
the Goldsmith debonair and wanton,

Saying, "O fine master, perfect in knowledge,
thy perfection is famous in all lands.

Lo, such and such a King hath chosen thee
for thy skill in the goldsmith's craft, because
thou art eminent.

Look now, receive these robes of honour and
gold and silver: when thou comest to the
King, thou wilt be his favourite and boon
companion."

The man saw the much wealth and the many
robes: he was beguiled, he parted from his
town and children.

Blithely he set out on the road, unaware that
the King had formed a design against his life.

He mounted an Arab horse and sped on joy-
ously: he deemed a robe of honour what
really was the price of his blood.

O fool, so willingly with thine own feet to enter
on the journey to thy doom!

In his fancy were dreams of riches, power, and
lordship. Said Azrael,[1] "Go thy way: yes,
thou wilt get them!"

[1] The Angel of Death.

9

Proudly and delicately they conducted him to the King, that he might burn like a moth on that candle of Tarāz.[1]

The King beheld him, showed great regard for him, and entrusted to him the treasure house full of gold.

Then the Physician said, "O mighty Sultan, give thy handmaiden to this master,

That she may be happy with him and that the water of union may quench the fire of passion."

The King bestowed on him that moon-faced one and wedded the twain who craved each other's company.

During the space of six months they satisfied their desires, till the girl was wholly restored to health.

Afterwards, he prepared a potion for him, so that he began to dwindle away.

When because of sickness his beauty remained not, the soul of the girl remained not in his deadly toils.

Since he appeared ugly and ill-favoured and sallow-cheeked, little by little he became unpleasing to her heart.

Those loves which are for the sake of a colour are not love: in the end they are a disgrace.

[1] This expression is applied to persons of resplendent beauty, like the women of Tarāz in Turkistan.

Would that he too had lacked all grace, that
such an evil doom might not have come to
pass upon him!

Blood ran from his eye like a river: his hand-
some face had become an enemy to his life.

The peacock's plumage is its enemy. How many
a king hath been slain by his magnificence!

He said, "I am the muskdeer whose gland
caused the hunter to shed its innocent blood,

Or the fox of the field for which they lay in wait
to cut off its head for the sake of the fur,

Or the elephant whose blood was shed by the
mahout for the sake of the ivory.

He who hath slain me for that which is not
myself,[1] does not he know that my blood
sleepeth not?

To-day the doom is on me, to-morrow it is on
him: how should the blood of one like me
rest unavenged?

Although the wall casts a long shadow, yet at
last the shadow turns back again towards it.

The world is the mountain, and our action the
shout: the echo of the shout comes back to
us."

With these words he gave up the ghost. The
Handmaiden was purged of love and pain,

Because love of the dead is not enduring, for the
dead are never coming back to us;

[1] *i.e.* for my beauty.

While love of the living is always fresher than a bud in the spirit and in the sight.

Choose the love of that Living One, who is everlasting and gives thee to drink of the wine that increases life.

Choose the love of Him from whose love all the prophets gained power and glory.

Do not say, "We have no admission to that King." Dealings with the generous are not difficult.

II

THE GROCER AND THE PARROT[1]

THERE was a Grocer who had a parrot, a sweet-
voiced, green, talking parrot.

Perched on the bench, it would watch over the
shop in its master's absence and talk to the
customers.

Once, as it sprang from the bench and flew
away, it spilled some bottles of rose-oil.

Its master came from his house and merchant-
wisé seated himself at ease on the bench.

Finding the bench wet with oil and his clothes
greasy, he smote the parrot on the head: it
was made bald by the blow.

For some few days it refrained from speech;
the Grocer, repenting, heaved deep sighs

And tore his beard, saying, "Alas, the sun of
my prosperity is gone under the clouds.

Would that my hand had been paralysed when
I struck such a blow on the head of that
sweet-tongued one!"

He was giving presents to every dervish, that
he might get back the speech of his bird.

[1] Book I, *v.* 247. This story illustrates the folly of reason-
ing by analogy (*qiyās*) and judging by appearances.

After three days and nights he was seated on
the bench, distraught and sorrowful like a
man in despair,

Showing the bird all sorts of marvels, that perchance it might begin to speak,

When a bare-headed dervish passed by, clad in
a *jawlaq*, his head hairless as the outside of a
bowl.

Thereupon the parrot began to talk, screeched
at the dervish, and said, "Hey, fellow!

How were you mixed up with the bald, O bald-
pate? Did you, then, spill oil from a bottle?"

The bystanders laughed at the parrot's infer-
ence, because it deemed the wearer of the
frock to be like itself.

III

THE MAN WHO FLEW TO HINDUSTĀN[1]

ONE morn, to Solomon in his hall of justice
A noble suitor came, running in haste,
His countenance pale with anguish, his lips blue.
"What ails thee, Khwāja?" asked the King.
  Then he:
"'Twas Azrael—ah, such a look he cast
On me of rage and vengeance." "Come now, ask
What boon thou wilt." "Protector of our lives,
I pray thee, bid the Wind convey me straight
To Hindustān: thy servant, there arrived,
Shall peradventure save his soul from Death."

How folk do ever flee from dervishhood
Into the jaws of greed and idle hope!
Your fear of dervishhood is that doomed man's
  terror,
Greed and ambition are your Hindustān.

Solomon bade the Wind convey him swiftly
Over the sea to farthest Hindustān.
On the morrow, when the King in audience
  sate,

[1] Book I, *v.* 956.

He said to Azrael, "Wherefore didst thou look
Upon that Musulmān so wrathfully,
His home knew him no more?" "Nay, not in
    wrath,"
Replied the Angel, "did I look on him;
But seeing him pass by, I stared in wonder,
For God had bidden me take his soul that day
In Hindustān. I stood there marvelling.
Methought, even if he had a hundred wings,
'Twere far for him to fly to Hindustān."

Judge all things of the world by this same rule
And ope your eyes and see! Away from whom
Shall we run headlong? From ourselves?
    Absurd!
Whom take ourselves away from? God? O
    crime!

THE SŪFĪ AND THE UNFAITHFUL
SERVANT[1]

ONE night a wandering Sūfī became a guest at a
monastery for dervishes.

He tied his ass in the stable; then he joined the
brethren on the dais,

Who were engaged in devotional meditation:
the friend of God is a better companion than
a book.

The Sūfī's book does not consist of ink and
letters: it is naught but a heart white as snow.

When at last the meditation of those godly
Sūfīs came to an end in ecstasy and enthusiasm

They furnished the guest with food, and he
then bethought him of his ass.

He said to the servant, "Go into the stable and
provide straw and barley for the beast."

"God help us!"[2] he replied, "why talk too
much? This has been my job for ever so
long."

[1] Book II, *v.* 156. The Unfaithful Servant represents the
Devil and the religious hypocrite.

[2] *Lā hawl*, "there is no power (or strength except in God
Almighty)."

The Sūfī said, "First wet the barley, for 'tis an old ass, and his teeth are shaky."

"God help us!" said he. "Why are you telling this to me, Sir? I am the one to give instructions."

The Sūfī said, "After having taken off his saddle put the *manbal* salve on his sore back."

"God help us!" exclaimed the servant. "Why, O purveyor of wisdom, I have had a thousand guests of your sort,

And all have departed from us well pleased: our guests are dear to us as our kinsfolk and as life itself."

The Sūfī said, "Give him water, but let it be lukewarm." "God help us!" cried the other. "I am ashamed of you."

The Sūfī said, "Put a little straw in his barley." "God help us! Cut short this palaver," he replied.

The Sūfī said, "Sweep his place clear of stones and dung, and if it is damp, sprinkle some dry earth on it."

"God help us!" cried he. "Implore God's help, O father, and don't waste words on a messenger who knows his business."

The Sūfī said, "Take the comb and curry his back." "God help us! Do have some shame, O father," said he.

Then, briskly girding up his loins, "I go,"

said he; "first I will fetch the straw and
barley."

Off he went and never gave a thought to the
stable: he beguiled the Sūfī with the sleep
of the hare.[1]

The servant went off to some rascally friends
and made a mockery of the Sūfī's admonition.

The Sūfī was fatigued by his journey and lay
down: with eyes closed he was dreaming

That his ass had fallen into the clutch of a wolf
which was tearing its back and thighs.

"God help us!" he exclaimed. "What melan-
choly madness is this? Oh, where is that
kindly servant?"

Again, he would see his ass going along the
road and tumbling now into a well and now
into a ditch.

He was dreaming unpleasant dreams, he was
reciting the *Fātiha*[2] and the *Qāri'a*.[3]

He asked himself, "What can be done? My
friends have hurried out and left all the doors
locked."

Again he would say, "Oh, I wonder—that
wretched servant! Did not he partake of
bread and salt with us?

---

[1] *i.e.* he caused the Sūfī to imagine that he (the Servant)
was wide-awake and attentive, though he was really like the
hare, which sleeps with its eyes open.

[2] The opening chapter of the *Qur'ān*.

[3] The hundred-and-first chapter of the *Qur'ān*.

19

I showed him nothing but courtesy: why should
he behave despitefully to me?

There must be a cause for every hatred; our
common humanity inspires feelings of friendship."

But then he would think, "When did Adam,
the kind and generous, do an injury to
Iblis?[1]

What was done by man to snake and scorpion
that they seek to inflict death and pain upon
him?

To rend is the instinct of the wolf: after all,
envy is conspicuous in mankind."

Again he would say, "It is wrong to think evil:
why should I bear such thoughts against my
brother?"

But then he would reflect that prudence consists in thinking evil: how shall he that thinks
no evil remain unhurt?

So deep was the Sūfī's anxiety, and meanwhile
his ass was in such a plight that—may it
befall our enemies!

The poor ass lay amidst earth and stones, with
his saddle awry and his halter torn,

Wellnigh killed by fatigue, without fodder all
the night long, now at the last gasp and now
perishing.

All night the ass was repeating, "O God, I give

[1] Satan. The word is a corruption of $\delta\iota\acute{\alpha}\beta o\lambda o\varsigma$.

up the barley, but am I not to have even a handful of straw?"

With mute eloquence he was saying, "O Shaykhs, have pity, for I am consumed with anguish because of this rude, impudent rogue."

All night till dawn the miserable ass rolled on his side, tormented by hunger.

At daybreak the servant came and instantly set the saddle straight on his back,

And after the fashion of ass-dealers gave him two or three blows with a goad: he did to the ass what suited a cur like him.

The sharp pricks made the ass jump up—hath an ass speech to describe his feelings?

When the Sūfī mounted him and got going, the ass began to fall on his face again and again,

And the travellers lifted him up every time: they all thought something was wrong.

One would twist his ears hard, while another sought for the laceration under his palate,

And another searched for the stone in his shoe, and another looked for the dirt in his eye.

"O Shaykh," they asked, "what is the cause of this? Didn't you say yesterday, 'Thank God, the ass is in fine fettle'?"

The Sūfī replied, "The ass that lived all night

on 'God help us!' cannot get along except in this manner.

Since his only food was 'God help us' he was praying to God by night and is prostrating himself by day."

V

THE FALCON AMONGST THE OWLS[1]

THE Falcon is he that comes back to the King.
    He that has lost the way is the blind falcon.
It lost the way and fell into the wilderness;[2]
    then in the wilderness it fell amongst owls.[3]
The Falcon is wholly light emanating from the
    Light of Divine Grace, but Destiny hath
    blinded it,
Thrown dust in its eyes and led it far from the
    right way and left it amongst the owls in the
    wilderness.
To crown all, the owls attack it and tear its
    lovely wing-feathers and plumes.
A clamour arose amongst the owls—"Ha! the
    Falcon hath come to seize our dwelling-
    place."[4]
'Twas as when the street-dogs, wrathful and
    terrifying, have fallen upon the frock of a
    strange dervish.

[1] Book II, *v.* 1131. The Falcon is a type of the righteous
man, and particularly the prophet or saint, whose heart is
turned to God.
[2] The world.
[3] Worldlings.
[4] The unbelievers asserted that the prophets were seeking
power and wealth for themselves.

23

"How am I fit," says the Falcon, "to consort with owls? I give up to the owls a hundred wildernesses like this.

I do not wish to stay here, I am going, I will return to the King of kings.

O ye owls, do not kill yourselves with agitation! I am not settling here, I am going home.

This ruin seems a thriving abode to you, but my pleasure-seat is the King's wrist."

"Beware," said the great Owl to his friends, "the Falcon is plotting to uproot you from house and home.

He will seize our houses by his cunning, he will then turn us out of our nests by his hypocrisy.

He boasts of the King and the King's wrist in order that he may lead us astray, simpletons as we are!

How should a petty bird be familiar with the King? Do not hearken to him, if ye have any understanding.

As for his saying, from deceit and feint and artifice, 'The King with all his retinue is searching after me,'

Here's an absurd mad fancy for you, here's a vain brag and a snare to catch blockheads!

If the smallest owl strike at his brain, where is succour for him from the King?"

The Falcon said, "If a single feather of mine

be broken, the King of kings will uproot the whole owlery.

An owl forsooth! Even if a falcon vex my heart and maltreat me,

The King will heap up in every hill and dale hundreds of thousands of stacks of falcons' heads.

His favour keeps watch over me: wherever I go, the King is following behind.

My image is abiding in the King's heart: sick would the King be without my image.

When the King bids me fly in His Way, I soar up to the heart's zenith, like His beams.

I fly as a moon and sun, I rend the curtains of the skies.

O blest is the owl that had the good fortune to apprehend my mystery!

Cling to me, that ye may rejoice and may become royal falcons, although ye are but owls.

I am the owner of the spiritual kingdom, I am not a lickspittle. The King is beating the falcon-drum for me from Beyond.

My falcon-drum is the call, 'Return!'[1] God is my witness in despite of adversary.

I am not a congener of the King of kings—far be it from Him!—but I have light from His radiance.

---

[1] *Qur'ān*, lxxxix, 27-28. "*O soul at peace, return to thy Lord, well pleased and well pleased with!*"

Since my *genus* is not the *genus* of my King, my
ego has passed away for the sake of His ego.

My ego has passed away, He remains alone: I
roll at the feet of His horse like the dust.

My individual self became dust, and the only
trace of it is the print of His feet upon its
dust.

Become dust at His feet for the sake of that
footprint, in order that ye may be as the
diadem on the head of the exalted.

Let not my puny form deceive you. Partake of
my banquet ere I depart."

VI

THE MAN WHO FANCIED HE SAW THE NEW MOON[1]

Once, in 'Umar's time, when the Month of
   Fast came round, some people ran to the top
   of a hill,
In order to have the luck of seeing the new
   moon;[2] and one of them said, "Look, there
   is the new moon, O 'Umar!"
As 'Umar did not see the moon in the sky, he said,
   "This moon has risen from thy imagination.
Otherwise, since I am a better observer of the
   heavens than thou art, how do I not see the
   pure crescent?
Wet thy hand and rub it on thine eyebrow, and
   then look for the new moon."

[1] Book II, v. 112.
[2] "The night on which Ramadān (the month of abstinence, the ninth month of the year) is expected to commence
is called 'Leylet er-Rooyeh,' or the Night of the Observation
[of the new moon]. In the afternoon, or earlier, during the
preceding day, several persons are sent a few miles into the
desert, where the air is particularly clear, in order to obtain
a sight of the new moon: for the fast commences on the
next day after the new moon has been seen. . . . The evidence of one Muslim, that he has seen the new moon, is
sufficient for the proclaiming of the fast." Lane, *The Modern
Egyptians*, ch. xxv.

27

When the man wetted his eyebrow, he could not see the moon. "O King," said he, "there is no moon; it has disappeared."

"Yes," said 'Umar, "the hair of thine eyebrow became a bow and shot at thee an arrow of false opinion."

One crooked hair had misled him, so that he vainly boasted to have seen the moon.

Inasmuch as a crooked hair veils the sky, how will it be if all your members are crooked?

Straighten your members by the help of the righteous. O you who would go straight, turn not aside from the door where the righteous dwell.

VII

THE BRAGGART AND THE SHEEP'S TAIL[1]

A PERSON, who on account of his poverty was lightly esteemed, used to grease his moustache every morning with the skin of a fat sheep's tail,

And go amongst the rich, saying, "I was at the party and had a good dinner."

He would gaily touch his moustache, meaning, "Look at it!

For it bears witness to the truth of my words, and is the token of my having eaten greasy and delicious food."

His belly would say in mute response, "May God confound the plots of the liars!

Thy boasting hath set me on fire: may thy greasy moustache be torn out!

Beggar that thou art! Were it not for thy foul bluster, some generous man would have taken pity on me.

If thou hadst shown the ailment and hadst not played false, some physician would have devised a remedy for it."

[1] Book III, *v.* 732.

His belly pleaded against his moustache and secretly had recourse to prayer,

Crying, "O God, expose this idle brag of the base, in order that the noble may be moved with pity towards me."

The belly's prayer was answered: the ardency of need produced a flame.[1]

God hath said, "Though thou be a profligate and idolater, I will answer when Thou callest Me."

Do thou cleave unto prayer and ever cry out: in the end it will deliver thee from the hands of the ghoul.

When the belly committed itself to God, the cat came and carried off the sheep's tail.

They pursued her, but she escaped. The braggart's child turned pale in fear of a scolding;

Nevertheless that little boy came into the midst of the company and destroyed his father's prestige.

"Father," said he, "the sheep's tail, with which you grease your lips and moustache every morning—

The cat came and suddenly snatched it away. I ran hard, but it was no use."

Those who were present laughed in astonishment, and their feelings of compassion were roused.

[1] Literally, "put forth a flag."

They invited him to eat and kept him well fed,
 they sowed the seed of pity in his soil;
And he, having tasted honesty from the noble,
 became humbly devoted to honesty.

VIII

THE THREE FISHES[1]

This, O obstinate man, is the story of the lake
in which there were three great fishes.

You will have read it in *Kalīla*,[2] but that is only
the husk of the story, while this is the spiritual
kernel.

Some fishermen passed by the lake and saw the
concealed prey.

They hastened to bring the net: the fishes
observed them and understood their inten-
tion.

The intelligent fish[3] resolved to migrate, he
resolved to make the difficult unwelcome
journey.

He said, "I will not consult these others, for
they will certainly weaken the strength of my
purpose.

Love for their native place holds sway over
their souls: their indolence and ignorance
will affect me too."

[1] Book IV, *v.* 2202.
[2] *Kalīla and Dimna*, the Arabic version of the Sanskrit
Pancha-tantra, made by Ibn al-Muqaffaʿ in the eighth century A.D.
[3] The Ṣūfī whose object is union with God.

For consultation, a goodly and spiritually living
  person is needed, so that he may endow thee
  with spiritual life; and where is that living one
  to be found?

O traveller, take counsel with a traveller, for a
  woman's counsel will make thy foot lame.

Pass beyond "love of country," do not stop at
  its outward sense. O soul, thy real country is
  Yonder, not here.

If thou desire thy country, cross to the other
  bank of the river. Do not misread the true
  Tradition of the Prophet.[1]

The wary fish swam away on his breast: he was
  going from his perilous abode towards the
  Sea of Light,

Like the deer which is pursued by a dog and
  keeps running so long as there is a single
  nerve in its body.

Hare's sleep[2] with the dog in pursuit is a sin;
  how indeed should sleep dwell in the eyes of
  him who hath fear?

That fish departed and took the way to the Sea:
  he chose the far way and illimitable expanse.

The second fish[3] said in the hour of tribulation,

---

[1] "Love of country is part of the Faith."

[2] The real heedlessness and indifference of one who super-
ficially has the appearance of being on his guard.

[3] A symbol of those who, lacking the perfect wisdom of
the prophet or saint, are wise enough to attach themselves
to a spiritual Guide and follow him on the Way to Salvation.

when he was left without the protection of
the intelligent one,

"He is gone to the Sea and is freed from sorrow:
my good comrade is lost to me.

But I will not think of that. Now I must attend
to myself. Let me feign to be dead

And turn my belly upwards and my back down-
wards and float on the water.

I will become dead, I will commit myself to
the water: to die before death[1] is to be safe
from torment."

To die before death is to be safe, O youth: even
so hath Mustafā[2] commanded us,

Who said, "Die, all of you, ere death come;
else ye will die in grievous affliction."

The second fish died in that manner and threw
his belly upwards: the water was carrying
him, now alow, now aloft.

The fishermen were exceedingly vexed and
cried, "Alas, the best fish is dead."

He rejoiced at their saying "Alas"; he thought
to himself, "My trick has come off, I am
delivered from the sword."

A worthy fisherman seized him and spat on him
and flung him to the ground.

Then the half-wise fish, rolling over and over,
slipped quietly into the water. Meanwhile

---

[1] The mystical death to self (*fanā*).
[2] Mohammed.

34

the foolish one[1] was darting to and fro in agitation.

That simpleton kept leaping about, right and left, in order that he might save his skin by his own efforts.

They cast the net, and he was caught in the net: his foolishness ensconced him in the fire of perdition.

On the top of the fire, on the surface of a frying-pan, he became the bedfellow of Folly.

There he was seething in the flames, while Reason asked, *"Did not a Warner come to thee?"*[2]

He, from the rack of torture and tribulation, was replying, like the souls of the unbelievers: *they said, "Yea."*

[1] The carnal man who has no light of his own and will not submit to be led by that of another.

[2] As the infidels shall be asked by the keepers of Hell on the Day of Judgment (*Qur'ān*, lxvii, 8).

IX

THE GREEK AND CHINESE ARTISTS[1]

THE Chinese said, "We have the greater skill";
the Greeks said, "The superior excellence
belongs to us."

"I will put you both to the test," said the Sultan, "and see which party makes good its
claim."

There were two rooms with door facing
door: the Chinese took one, the Greeks the
other.

The Chinese asked the Sultan for a hundred
colours: he opened his treasury that they
might receive them,

And every morning, by his bounty, the colours
were dispensed to the Chinese.

The Greeks said, "For our work no colours
are necessary: we need only remove the
rust."

They shut the door and began to burnish:
the walls became bright and pure like the
sky.

There is a way from many-colouredness to

[1] Book I, v. 3467.

36

colourlessness: colour is the cloud, colourlessness the moon.[1]

Whatsoever light and splendour you see in the
clouds, know that it comes from the stars and
the moon and the sun.

When the Chinese finished their work, they
beat drums in jubilation.

The Sultan entered and looked at the pictures:
their beauty almost robbed him of understanding.

Afterwards he visited the Greeks. They had
lifted the curtain between themselves and
the Chinese,

So that the Chinese paintings were reflected
upon those shining walls.

All that he had seen there seemed more beautiful here: 'twas drawing the eye from the
socket.

The Greeks, O father, are the Sūfīs. They are
without learning and books and erudition,

But they have burnished their hearts and
made them pure of greed and avarice and
hatred.

That pure mirror[2] is, beyond doubt, the heart
which receives images innumerable.

[1] Cf. Shelley's—
"Life, like a dome of many-coloured glass,
Stains the white radiance of eternity."
[2] *i.e.* the walls which the Greeks had polished.

The spiritual Moses[1] holds in his bosom the infinite form of the Unseen reflected from the mirror of his heart.[2]

[1] The illumined saint. There is an allusion to the command given to Moses on Mt. Sinai (*Qur'ān*, xxvii, 12; xxviii, 32), "*Thrust thy hand into thy bosom: it will come forth white without hurt.*"

[2] The Perfect Man is a microcosm in which all the divine attributes are reflected as in a mirror.

X

THE DRUGGIST AND THE CLAY-EATER[1]

A CLAY-EATER went to a druggist to buy a quantity of fine hard sugar-loaf.

The druggist, who was a crafty, vigilant man, informed his customer that the balance-weight was clay.[2]

"I want the sugar at once," replied the clay-eater; "let the weight be what you will."

He said to himself, "What does it matter to me? Clay is better than gold."

The druggist therefore put the clay, which he had ready, in one scale of the balance,

And began to break with his hand the equivalent amount of sugar for the other scale.

Since he had no pick-axe, he took a long time and kept the customer waiting.

Whilst he was busy with the sugar, the clay-

---

[1] Book IV, *v.* 625. The practice of geophagy is often mentioned in the *Mathnawī*. According to Schlimmer (*Terminologie médico-pharmaceutique*, Teheran, 1874, p. 299) it is common amongst Persian women. The province of Khurāsān gave its name to a brilliant white clay, which was eaten roasted; and there were other well-known varieties.

[2] Implying that it was deficient.

eater, unable to restrain his appetite, helped himself covertly to the clay,

In a terrible fright lest the druggist's eye should fall upon him of a sudden for the purpose of testing his honesty.

The druggist saw him but feigned to be busy, saying to himself, "Come, take some more, O pale-face.

If you will be a thief and filch my clay, go on, for you are eating out of your own side.

You are afraid of me, because you are a stupid ass; I am only afraid that you will eat too little.

Busy as I am, I am not such a fool as to let you get too much of my sugar.

When you see the amount of sugar you have bought, then you will know who was foolish and careless."

XI

THE FROZEN SNAKE[1]

A SNAKE-CATCHER went to the mountains to catch a snake by his incantations.

Whether one be slow or quick, he that is a seeker will be a finder.

Always apply yourself with both hands to seeking, for search is an excellent guide on the way.

Though you be lame and limping and bent in figure and unmannerly, ever creep towards God and be in quest of Him.

Now by speech, now by silence, and now by smelling, catch in every quarter the scent of the King.

Smell all the way from the part to the Whole, O noble one; smell all the way from opposite to opposite, O wise one.

Assuredly wars bring peace; the snake-catcher sought the snake for the purpose of friendship.

Man seeks a snake for his friend and cares for one that is without care for him.[2]

[1] Book III, v. 976.

[2] The snake, as the poet explains afterwards, is the sensual "self," which is Man's worst enemy.

The snake-catcher was searching in the mountains for a big snake in the days of snow.

He espied there a huge dead serpent, at the aspect whereof his heart was filled with fear.

The snake-catcher catches snakes in order to astonish the people—oh, the foolishness of the people!

Man is a mountain:[1] how should he be led into temptation? How should a mountain be astonished by a snake?

Wretched Man does not know himself: he has come from a high estate and fallen into lowlihood.

Man has sold himself cheaply: he was satin, he has patched himself on to a tattered cloak.

Hundreds of thousands of snakes and mountains are amazed at him: how, then, has he become amazed and in love with a snake?

The snake-catcher took up the serpent and came to Baghdād in order to excite astonishment.

For the sake of a paltry fee he carried along with him a serpent like the pillar of a house,

Saying, "I have brought a dead serpent: I have suffered agonies in hunting it."

He thought it was dead, but it was alive, and he had not inspected it very well.

[1] Man, created in the image of God, resembles a mountain in the grandeur and might of his essential nature.

It was frozen by frosts and snow; it was living, though it presented the appearance of the dead.

The World is frozen: its name is *jamād* (inanimate); *jāmid* means "frozen," O master.

Wait till the Sun of the Resurrection shall rise, that thou mayst see the movement of the World's body!

At last the would-be showman arrived at Baghdād, to set up a public show at the crossroads.

The man set up a show on the bank of the Tigris, and a great hubbub arose in the city—

"A snake-catcher has brought a serpent; he has captured a marvellous rare beast."

Myriads of simpletons assembled, who had become a prey to him as he to his folly.

They were waiting to see the serpent, and he too waited for them to assemble.

The greater the crowd, the better goes the begging and contributing of money.

Myriads of idle babblers gathered round, forming a ring, sole against sole.[1]

Men took no heed of women: all were mingled in the throng, like nobles and common folk at the Resurrection.

When he began to lift the cloth covering the serpent, the people strained their necks,

[1] *i.e.* standing closely packed together on tiptoe.

43

And saw that the serpent, which had been
frozen by intense cold, lay underneath a
hundred coarse woollen blankets and coverlets.

He had bound it with thick ropes: the careful
keeper had taken great precautions.

During the interval of expectation and coming
together, the sun of 'Irāq shone upon the
snake.

The sun of the hot country warmed it: the cold
humours went out of its limbs.

It was dead, and it revived: the astonished serpent began to uncoil itself.

By the stirring of the dead serpent the people's
amazement was increased a hundred thousandfold.

They fled, shrieking, while the cords binding the
serpent went crack, crack, one after another.

It burst the bonds and glided out from beneath
—a hideous dragon roaring like a lion.

Multitudes were killed in the rout: a hundred
heaps were made of the fallen slain.

The snake-catcher stood paralysed with fear,
crying, "What have I brought from the mountains and the desert?"

The blind sheep awakened the wolf and un-
wittingly went to meet its Azrael.

The serpent made one mouthful of that dolt:
blood-drinking is easy for a Hajjāj.

It wound itself on a pillar and crunched the
bones of the devoured man.

The serpent is thy carnal soul: how is it dead?
It is only frozen by grief and lack of means.
If it obtain the means of Pharaoh, by whose
command the Nile would flow,
Then it will begin to act like Pharaoh and waylay a hundred such as Moses and Aaron.
That serpent, under stress of poverty, is a little
worm; but a gnat is made a falcon by power
and riches.
Keep the serpent in the snow of separation from
its desires. Beware, do not carry it into the
sun of 'Irāq!

XII

THE SINCERE PENITENT[1]

A MAN was going to attend the Friday prayers:
    he saw the people leaving the mosque
And asked one of them why they were depart-
    ing so early.
He replied, "The Prophet has prayed with the
    congregation and finished his worship.
How art thou going in, O foolish person, after
    the Prophet has given the blessing?"
"Alas!" he cried; and it seemed as though the
    smell of his heart's blood issued, like smoke,
    from that burning sigh.
One of the congregation said, "Give me this
    sigh, and all my prayers are thine."
He answered, "I give thee the sigh and accept
    thy prayers." The other took the sigh that
    was so full of regret and longing.
At night, whilst he was asleep, a Voice said to
    him, "Thou hast bought the Water of Life
    and Salvation.
For the sake of that which thou hast chosen,
    the prayers of all the people have been ac-
    cepted."

[1] Book II, *v.* 2771.

XIII

THE PALADIN OF QAZWĪN[1]

Now hear a pleasant tale—and mark the scene—
About the way and custom of Qazwīn,
Where barbers ply their needles to tattoo
Folk's arms and shoulders with designs in blue.

Once a Qazwīnī spoke the barber fair:
"Tattoo me, please; make something choice
  and rare."
"What figure shall I paint, O paladin?"
"A furious lion: punch him boldly in.
Leo is my ascendant: come, tattoo
A lion, and let him have his fill of blue."
"On what place must I prick the deft design?"
"Trace it upon my shoulder, line by line."
He took the needle and dabbed and dabbed it
  in.
Feeling his shoulder smart, the paladin
Began to yell—"You have killed me quite, I
  vow:
What is this pattern you are doing now?"
"Why, sir, a lion, as you ordered me."
"Commencing with what limb?" demanded he.

[1] Book I, v. 2981.

"His tail," was the reply. "O best of men,
Leave out the tail, I beg, and start again.
The lion's tail and rump chokes me to death;
It's stuck fast in my windpipe, stops my
    breath.
O lion-maker, let him have no tail,
Or under these sharp stabs my heart will
    fail."
Another spot the barber 'gan tattoo,
Without fear, without favour, without rue.
"Oh, oh! which part of him is this? Oh
    dear!"
"This," said the barber, "is your lion's ear."
"Pray, doctor, not an ear of any sort!
Leave out his ears and cut the business short."
The artist quickly set to work once more:
Again our hero raised a doleful roar.
"On which third limb now is the needle em-
    ployed?"
"His belly, my dear sir." "Hold, hold!" he
    cried.
"Perish the lion's belly, root and branch!
How should the glutted lion want a paunch?"
Long stood the barber there in mute dismay,
His finger 'twixt his teeth; then flung away
The needle, crying, "All the wide world o'er
Has such a thing e'er happened heretofore?
Why, God Himself did never make, I tell ye,
A lion without tail or ears or belly!"

48

MORAL

Brother, endure the pain with patience fresh,
To gain deliverance from the miscreant flesh.
Whoso is freed from selfhood's vain conceit,
Sky, sun and moon fall down to worship at his
feet.

XIV

THE GREEDY INSOLVENT[1]

THERE was an Insolvent without house or
home, who remained in prison and pitiless
bondage.

He would unconscionably eat the rations of the
prisoners; on account of his appetite he lay
heavy as Mt. Qāf[2] on the hearts of the people
in the gaol.

No one durst eat a mouthful of bread, because
that food-snatcher would carry off his entire
meal.

The prisoners came to complain to the
Cadi's agent, who was possessed of discern-
ment,

Saying, "Take our salutations to the Cadi and
relate to him the sufferings inflicted on us
by this vile man;

For he is never out of prison, and he is a vaga-
bond, a lickspittle, and a nuisance.

Like a fly, he impudently presents himself at
every meal without invitation or salaam.

[1] Book II, v. 585.
[2] The inaccessible range of mountains by which, according
to Muslim belief, the earth is surrounded.

To him the food of sixty persons is nothing; he
  pretends to be deaf if you say 'Enough!'

Not a morsel reaches the ordinary prisoner,
  or if by a hundred shifts he discover some
  food,

That hell-throat at once comes forward with the
  argument that God has said, '*Eat ye.*'[1]

Justice, justice against such a three years'
  famine! May the shadow of our lord endure
  for ever!

Either let this buffalo out of prison, or make
  him a regular allowance of food from a trust-
  fund.

O thou by whom men and women are made
  happy, do justice! Thy help is invoked and
  besought."

The courteous agent went to the Cadi and
  related the complaint to him point by
  point.

The Cadi summoned the Insolvent to his presence, and inquired about him from his own
  officers.

All the complaints which the prisoners had set
  forth were proved to the Cadi.

The Cadi said to him, "Get up and depart from
  this prison: go to the house that belongs to
  you by inheritance."

---

[1] *Qur'ān*, vii, 29.

He replied, "My house and home consist in thy bounty; as in the case of an infidel, thy prison is my Paradise.[1]

If thou drive me from the prison and turn me out, I shall certainly die of beggary and destitution."

He pleaded like the Devil, who said, "*O Lord, grant me a respite till the Day of Resurrection,*[2]

For 'tis my pleasure to be in the prison of this World, so that I may slay the children of mine Enemy,

And, if anyone have some food of Faith and a single loaf as provision for the journey to the Life hereafter,

I may seize it by guile and cunning, and they in sorrow may raise an outcry of lamentation,

While sometimes I threaten them with poverty, and sometimes bind their eyes with the spell of tress and mole."

The Cadi said, "Prove that you are insolvent."
"Here are the prisoners," he replied, "as my witnesses."

[1] The Prophet is reported to have said, "This world is the infidel's Paradise."

[2] *Qur'ān*, vii, 13, slightly altered.

"They," said the Cadi, "are suspect, because they are fleeing from you and weeping blood on account of you;

They are suing for deliverance from you: by reason of self-interest their testimony is worthless."

All the people of the court said, " We bear witness both to his insolvency and his moral degeneracy."

Everyone whom the Cadi questioned about his condition said, "My lord, wash thy hands of this Insolvent."

Then said the Cadi, "March him round the city for all to see, and cry, 'This man is an insolvent and a great rogue.

Let no one sell to him on credit, let no one lend him a farthing.

Whatever charge of fraud may be brought against him, I will not commit him to prison in future.[1]

His insolvency has been proven to me: he possesses nothing, neither money nor goods.'"

When the show[2] started, they brought along the camel of a Kurd who sold firewood.

He made a great row, but all in vain, though he

---

[1] According to Muslim law, a debtor whose insolvency has been proven is not liable to imprisonment.

[2] *i.e.* the preparations for parading the Insolvent.

conciliated the police officer with the gift of a *dāng*.[1]

Upon the camel was seated that sore famine,[2] while the owner ran at its heels.

They sped from quarter to quarter and from street to street, till the whole town knew him by sight.

Ten loud-voiced criers, Turks and Kurds and Greeks and Arabs, made the following proclamation:

"This man is insolvent and has nothing: let no one lend him a brass farthing;

He does not possess a single mite, patent or latent; he is a bankrupt, a piece of falsehood, a cunning knave, an oil-bag.

Beware! Beware! Have no dealings with him: when he brings the ox to sell, tie up your money;

And if ye bring this decayed wretch for judgement, I will not imprison a corpse."

At nightfall, when the Insolvent dismounted, the Kurd said to him, "I live a long way off.

You have been riding on my camel since morning. Never mind the barley,[3] but at least give me what will pay for the straw."

[1] About a farthing.
[2] The Insolvent.
[3] *i.e.* "I don't ask you to pay me in full."

54

"Why," he rejoined, "what were we doing all day? Where are your wits? Is none of them at home?

My insolvency has been drummed up to the Seventh Heaven, but you have not heard the bad news!

Your ears were filled with foolish hope. Such hope makes one deaf and blind, my lad."

XV

JOSEPH AND HIS GUEST[1]

THE loving friend came from the ends of the
earth and became the guest of Joseph the
truthful;

For they had been friends in childhood, reclining together on the cushion of acquaint-
ance.

He spoke of the injustice and envy of Joseph's
brethren. Joseph said, "That was a chain,
and I was the lion.

The lion is not disgraced by the chain: I do not
complain of God's decree."

After Joseph had told him his story, he said,
"Now, O such and such, what traveller's gift
hast thou brought for me?

Come, produce it." At this demand the guest
sobbed aloud in confusion.

"How many a gift," he said, "did I seek for
thee! but no worthy gift came into my
sight.

How should I bring a grain of gold to the mine?
How should I bring a drop of water to the
sea?

[1] Book I, *v.* 3157.

56

I should only bring cumin to Kirmān[1] if I brought my heart and soul as a gift to thee.

There is no grain that is not in this barn except thy incomparable beauty.

I deemed it fitting that I should bring to thee a mirror like the inward light of a pure heart,

That thou mayst behold thy beauteous face therein, O thou who, like the sun, art the lamp of heaven.

I have brought thee a mirror, O light of mine eyes, so that when thou seest thy face thou mayst think of me."

---

[1] To "bring cumin to Kirmān" (in Southern Persia) means the same thing as "carrying coals to Newcastle."

XVI

THE MAN WHO TRUSTED THE BEAR[1]

A DRAGON was pulling a Bear into its jaws: a
   valiant man went and succoured it.

When it was delivered from the Dragon, it
   followed its benefactor like the dog of the
   Seven Sleepers.[2]

He, being fatigued, lay down to rest: the Bear,
   from devotion to him, became his guard.

A holy man passed by and said to him, "What
   is the matter? What has this Bear to do with
   thee, O brother?"

He related his adventure with the Dragon.
   "Fool!" said the other, "do not set thy heart
   on a bear."

The man thought to himself, "He is envious";
   then he said aloud, "See how fond of me it is!"

"The fondness of fools is deceiving," he replied;
   "my envy is better for thee than its affection.

---

[1] Book II, v. 1932.

[2] The *Qur'ān*, ch. xviii, relates the legend of the seven
Christian youths of Ephesus who, in the reign of the Emperor Decius, fled from persecution and took refuge in a
cave, where they slept for three hundred and nine years.
The dog which accompanied them (*vv.* 17 and 21) is said by
some to have had the name *ar-Raqīm* (*v.* 8); but this identi-
fication is very doubtful.

Drive the Bear away and come with me, do not
   make friends with the Bear, do not forsake
   one of thy own kind.
I am not less than a bear, O noble sir: abandon
   it in order that I may be thy comrade.
My heart is trembling for thee: do not go into
   a forest with a bear like this.
My heart has never trembled in vain; this is
   the Light of God, not pretence or idle
   boasting.
I am the true believer who sees by the Light of
   God.[1] Beware, beware! Flee from this fire-
   temple!"[2]
He said all this, but it entered not into his ear.
   Suspicion is a mighty barrier to a man.
"Go," cried he, "be not troubled for me, don't
   retail so much wisdom, O busybody."
He answered, saying, "I am not thy enemy: it
   would be a kindness if thou wouldst come
   with me."
"I am sleepy," said he; "let me alone; go!"

That Muslim left the foolish man and returned
   to his abode, muttering, "God help us!"
The man fell asleep, and the Bear kept driving
   the flies away from his face, but they soon
   came hurrying back again.

[1] As is declared in a Tradition of the Prophet.
[2] *i.e.* the *ignis fatuus* of carnality and vain desire.

The Bear went off in a rage and picked up a
very big stone from the mountain-side.

He fetched the stone, and seeing the flies again
settled on the face of his friend,

He took it up and struck at them to make them
go away.

The stone made powder of the sleeping man's
face and published to the whole world this
adage—

"Surely the love of a Fool is the love of a Bear:
his hate is love and his love is hate."

XVII

THE THIEF WHO SAID HE WAS A DRUMMER[1]

HEAR this parable—how a wicked Thief was cutting a hole at the bottom of a wall.

Someone who was ill and half awake heard the tapping of his pick.

And went on the roof and hung his head down and said to him, "What are you about, O father?

All is well, I hope. What are you doing here at midnight?

Who are you?" He said, "A drummer, O honourable sir."

"What are you about?" "I am beating the drum."

The sick man said, "Where is the noise of the drum, O artful one?"

He replied,"You will hear it to-morrow, namely, cries of 'Oh, alas!' and 'Oh, woe is me'!"

[1] Book III, *v.* 2799.

XVIII

THE GOLDSMITH WHO LOOKED AHEAD[1]

A CERTAIN man came to a Goldsmith, saying,
"Give me the scales that I may weigh some
gold."

He replied, "Go, I have no sieve." "Give me
the scales," said the other, "and don't waste
time in jesting."

"There is no broom in the shop," said the
Goldsmith. "Enough! Enough!" he exclaimed; "leave these jokes.

Give me the scales I am asking for. Don't pretend to be deaf; don't talk at random."

He replied, "I heard what you said, I am not
deaf; you must not think I am nonsensical.

I heard your request, but you are a shaky old
man: your hand trembles and your body is
bowed;

And moreover your gold consists of tiny filings,
which will drop from your trembling hand.

Then you will say, 'Sir, fetch a broom, that I
may search in the dust for my gold';

[1] Book III, v. 1624.

And when you have gathered the sweepings, you will tell me that you want the sieve.
I from the beginning discerned the end complete. Go from here to some other place, and farewell!"

XIX

LUQMĀN AND HIS MASTER[1]

LUQMĀN was the favourite of his master, who
preferred him to his own sons,
Because Luqmān, though a slave, was master
of himself and free from sensual desire.
A certain King said to a holy man, "Ask a boon
that I may bestow it upon thee."
He answered, "O King, are not you ashamed
to say such a thing to me? Mount higher!
I have two slaves, and they are vile, and
yet those twain are rulers and lords over
you."
Said the King, "Who are those twain? Surely
this is an error." He replied, "The one is
anger and the other is lust."

Luqmān was always the first to partake of any
viands that were served to his master,
For the master would send them to him, and if
Luqmān left them untasted his master would
throw them away;
Or, if he did eat of them, it would be without

[1] Book II, v. 1462.

64

heart and without appetite: this is the sign
of an affinity without end.

One day he received the gift of a melon. "Go,"
said he, "call hither my dear Luqmān."

He gave him a slice: Luqmān ate it as though
it were sugar and honey,

And showed such pleasure that his master went
on giving him slice after slice, seventeen in all.

One slice remained. He said, "I will eat this
myself, to see what a sweet melon it is."

No sooner had he tasted it than its sourness
blistered his tongue and burnt his throat.

For a while he was almost beside himself;
then he cried, "O Luqmān, my soul and my
world,

How could you have the patience? What made
you endure so long? Or perhaps life is hateful
to you."

Luqmān said, "From thy bounteous hand I
have eaten so many sweets that I am bent
double with shame.

I was ashamed to refuse one bitter thing from
thy hand, O wise master.

Since all parts of me have grown from thy
bounty and are a prey to thy bait and snare—

If I complain of one bitter thing, may the dust
of a hundred roads cover every part of me!

This melon had reposed in thy sugar-bestow-
ing hand: how could it retain any bitterness?"

Through Love bitter things become sweet;
through Love pieces of copper become golden.
Through Love dregs become clear; through
Love pains become healing.
Through Love the dead is made living; through
Love the king is made a slave.

XX

THE LION AND THE BEASTS OF CHASE[1]

THE Beasts of Chase in a pleasant valley were
  harassed by a Lion,
So they made a plan: they came to the Lion,
  saying, "We will keep thee full-fed by a fixed
  allowance.
Do not exceed thy allowance, else this pasture
  will become bitter to us."
"Yes," said he, "if I find good faith on your
  part, for I have suffered many a fraud at the
  hands of Zayd and Bakr.[2]
I am done to death by the cunning of man, I
  am stung by human snake and scorpion.
'The believer is not bitten twice': I have taken
  this saying of the Prophet to my heart."
The Beasts said, "O sagacious one, let precaution
  alone: it is of no avail against the divine Decree.
Precaution is but trouble and woe: put thy
  trust in God, trust in God is better.
O fierce Lion, do not grapple with Destiny lest
  Destiny pick a quarrel with thee."

[1] Book I, v. 900.
[2] Equivalent to "Tom, Dick, and Harry."

"Yes," he said; "but though trust in God is the true guide, yet we should use precaution according to the Prophet's rule.

The Prophet spoke plainly, saying, 'Trust in God, and bind the knee of thy camel.'

He hath also said, 'God loves the worker.' Let us trust in God, but not so as to neglect ways and means."

The Beasts answered him, saying, "There is no work better than trust in God: what indeed is dearer to Him than resignation?

Man contrives, and his contrivance is a snare to catch him: that which he thought would save his life sheds his blood.

He locks the door whilst his foe is in the house: the plot of Pharaoh was a tale of this kind.

We are the family of the Lord; like infants, we crave after milk.

God who gives rain from heaven is also able, in His mercy, to give us bread."

"Yes," said the Lion; "but the Lord hath set a ladder before our feet.

Step by step we must climb to the roof: to be a Necessitarian here is to indulge in foolish hopes.

You have feet: why do you pretend to be lame? You have hands: why do you hide your fingers?

When the master puts a spade in his slave's

hand, he need not speak in order to make his object known."

The Lion gave many proofs in this style, so that those Necessitarians became tired of answering him.

Fox and deer and hare and jackal abandoned their doctrine and ceased from disputation.

They made a covenant with the Lion, ensuring that he should incur no loss in the bargain,

And that he should receive his daily rations without trouble or any further demand.

Every day the one on whom the lot fell would run to the Lion as swiftly as a cheetah.

When the fatal cup came round to the Hare, "Why," cried the Hare, "how long shall we endure injustice?"

His companions said, "All this time we have sacrificed our lives in truth and loyalty.

Do not thou give us a bad name, O rebellious one! Quick! Quick! lest the Lion be aggrieved."

"O my friends," said he, "grant me a respite, that by my cunning ye may escape from this woe

And save your lives and leave security as a heritage to your children."

The Beasts replied, "O donkey, listen to us. Keep thyself within the measure of a hare!

Eh, what brag is this? Thy betters never thought of such a thing."

"My friends," said he, "God hath inspired me.
Weak as I am, I am wisely counselled.

God opens the door of knowledge to the bee,
so that it builds a house of honey.

God teaches the silkworm a craft beyond the
power of the elephant.

When Adam, the earth-born, gained knowledge of God, his knowledge illumined the
Seventh Heaven."

They said, "O nimble Hare, disclose what is
in thy mind. The Prophet hath said, 'Take
counsel with the trustworthy.'"

"Not every secret may be told," said he; "sometimes an even number turns out odd and an
odd one even.

If you breathe the hidden word on a mirror,
the mirror immediately becomes dim.

Hold your tongue concerning three things:
your departure, your money, and your religion."

The Hare tarried long, rehearsing to himself
the trick he was about to play.

At last he took the road and set forth to whisper
a few secrets in the Lion's ear.

The Lion, incensed and wrathful and frantic,
saw the Hare coming from afar,

Running undismayed and confidently, looking
angry and fierce and fell and sour;

For by appearing humble he thought suspicion would be excited, while boldness would remove every cause of doubt.

As soon as he approached, the Lion roared, "Ha, villain!

I who tear oxen limb from limb, I who bruise the ears of the raging elephant—

What! shall a half-witted hare presume to spurn my commands?"

"Mercy!" cried the Hare. "I have an excuse, please thy Majesty."

"What excuse?" said he. "O the shortsightedness of fools! Is this the time for them to come into the presence of kings?

The fool's excuse is worse than his crime, 'tis the poison that kills wisdom."

"Hark!" cried the Hare, "if I am not worthy of thy clemency, I will lay my head before the dragon of thy vengeance.

At breakfast-time I set out with another hare which the Beasts of Chase had appointed, for thy sake, to accompany me.

On the road a lion attacked thy humble slave, attacked both the companions in travel hastening towards thee.

I said to him, 'We are the slaves of the King of kings, two lowly fellow-servants of that exalted Court.'

He said, 'The King of kings! Who is he? Be

ashamed! Do not make mention of every base loon in my presence.

Both thee and thy King I will tear to pieces if thou and thy friend turn back from my portal.'

I said, 'Let me behold the face of my King once more and acquaint him with the news of thee.'

'Thou must leave thy comrade with me as a pledge,' said he; 'otherwise thy life is forfeit according to my law.'

We entreated him much: 'twas no use. He seized my friend and left me to go my way alone.

My friend was so big and plump and comely that he would make three of me.

Henceforth the road is barred by that lion: the cord of our covenant is broken.

Abandon hope of thy rations henceforward! I am telling thee the bitter truth.

If thou want the rations, clear the road! Come on, then, and drive away that insolent usurper!"

"Come on in God's name," cried the Lion. "Show me where he is! Lead the way, if you are speaking the truth,

That I may give him and a hundred like him the punishment they deserve—or do the same to you if you are lying."

The Hare set off, running ahead in the direction of a deep well which was to be a snare for the Lion;

But as they drew nigh to it, the Hare shrunk back. "That lion," said he, "lives here.

I am consumed with dread of his fury—unless thou wilt take me beside thee,

That with thy support, O Mine of generosity, I may open my eyes and look in."

The Lion took him to his side; they ran together towards the well and looked in.

The Lion saw his own reflection: from the water shone the image of a lion with a plump hare beside him.

No sooner did he espy his adversary than he left the Hare and sprang into the well.

He fell into the well which he had dug: his iniquity recoiled on his own head.

The Lion saw himself in the well: he was so enraged that he could not distinguish himself from his enemy.

O Reader, how many an evil that you see in others is but your own nature reflected in them!

In them appears all that you are—your hypocrisy, iniquity, and insolence.

You do not see clearly the evil in yourself, else you would hate yourself with all your soul.

Like the Lion who sprang at his image in the water, you are only hurting yourself, O simpleton!

When you reach the bottom of the well of your own nature, then you will know that the wickedness is in *you*.

XXI

THE SŪFĪ AND THE EMPTY WALLET[1]

ONE day a Sūfī espied a food-wallet hanging on a nail; he began to whirl in the dance and rend his garments,

Crying, "Lo, the food of the foodless! Lo, the remedy for famine and pangs of hunger!"

When his smoke and tumult waxed great, every one that was a Sūfī joined him.

They all shouted and shrieked and became spiritually intoxicated and beside themselves.

An idle busybody said to the Sūfī, "What is the matter? Only a food-wallet hung on a nail, and it is empty of bread."

"Begone, begone!" he replied. "Thou art a mere form without spirit. Go, seek existence,[2] for thou art no lover."

The lover's food is love of the bread, without the existence of the bread. No true lover is in thrall to existence.

[1] Book III, v. 3014.
[2] i.e. self-existence with all its egoistic wants and desires, which is regarded by the lover of God as the greatest sin.

75

Lovers have naught to do with existence: lovers have the interest without having the capital. They have no wings, and yet they fly round the world; they have no hands, and yet they carry off the ball from the polo-field.

XXII

THE DIFFERENCE BETWEEN FEELING
AND THINKING[1]

SOMEONE slapped Zayd on the neck; Zayd
rushed at him with warlike purpose.

The assailant said, "I will ask thee a question.
First answer it, and then strike me.

I smote the nape of thy neck, and there was
the sound of a slap. At this point I have a
friendly question to ask thee.

Was the sound caused by my hand or by the
nape of thy neck, O pride of the noble?"

Zayd said, "On account of the pain I have no
time to reflect on this problem.

Do thou who art without pain reflect on it;
he that feels the pain cannot think of such
things."

---

[1] Book III, v. 1380. This is the second of two apologues
illustrating the attitude of emotional mysticism towards
scholastic theology. The first story concerns an elderly man
who was about to be married. He went to a barber and bade
him remove the white hairs in his beard, whereupon the
barber cut off the whole beard, laid it before his customer,
and said to him, "Pick them out yourself, I have important
business to attend to."

XXIII

THE GNAT AND THE WIND[1]

THE Gnat came from the garden and the grass
and appealed to Solomon,

Saying, "O Solomon, thou dealest justice to
the devils and the children of men and the
genii.

Bird and fish are protected by thy justice:
where is the wretch whom thy bounty has
not sought out?

Give justice to us, for we are very miserable:
we are deprived of the orchard and rose-
garden.

The difficulties of every weakling are solved
by thee: the Gnat in sooth is a proverb for
weakness.

O thou who hast reached the limit in Power,
while we have reached the limit in failure
and aberration,

Do justice, relieve us of this sorrow, support
us, O thou whose hand is the hand of
God."

Then Solomon asked, "Against whom art thou
demanding justice and equity, O suitor?

[1] Book III, v. 4624.

Who is the tyrant that in his insolence has done
thee injury and scratched thy face?

Oh, wonderful! Where, in Our epoch, is the
oppressor that is not in Our prison and
chains?

When We were born, on that day Injustice
died: who, then, has committed in Our epoch
an act of injustice?

The Divine Will uttered in '*Be, and it was*'
hath bestowed the Kingdom on Us, that
the people may not cry in lament to
Heaven;

That burning sighs may not soar upward; that
the sky and the stars may not be shaken;

That the empyrean may not tremble at the
orphan's wail; that no living soul may be
marred by violence.

O oppressed one, do not look to Heaven, for
thou hast a heavenly King in the temporal
world."

"I appeal," said the Gnat, "against the fury of
the Wind, for he hath opened the hands of
oppression against us.

Through his oppression we are in sore straits:
with closed lips we are drinking blood."[1]

Said Solomon, "O thou with the pretty voice,
it behoves thee to hearken with all thy soul
to the command of God,

[1] *i.e.* suffering torment.

God hath said to me, 'Beware, O Judge! Do not
hear one litigant without the other.

Until both litigants come into the presence, the
truth does not come to light before the
judge.'

I dare not avert my face from the Divine
command. Go, bring thy adversary before
me."

"Thy words," said the Gnat, "are an argument
conclusive and sound. My adversary is the
Wind, and he is at thy behest."

The King shouted, "O Wind, the Gnat com-
plains of thy injustice. Come!

Hark, come face to face with thy adversary and
reply to him and rebut him."

When the Wind heard the summons, he came
rapidly: the Gnat at once took to flight.

"O Gnat," cried Solomon, "where art thou
going? Stop, that I may pass judgement upon
you both."

The Gnat answered, "O King, his being is my
death; verily, my day is made black by his
smoke.

Since he has come, where shall I find peace?
He wrings the vital breath out of my
body."

Even such is the seeker at the Court of God:
when God comes, the seeker is naughted.

Although union with God is life on life, yet at
    first that life consists in dying to self.
The shadows that seek the Light are naughted
    when His Light appears.
How should reason remain when He bids it go?
    Everything is perishing except His Face.[1]

[1] *Qur'ān*, xxviii, 88.

XXIV

THE PRINCE WHO WAS BEATEN AT CHESS BY THE COURT-JESTER[1]

THE Prince of Tirmidh was playing chess with Dalqak. When Dalqak mated him, his anger burst.

On hearing the word "Checkmate!" the haughty monarch threw the chessmen, one by one, at Dalqak's head.

"Here, take your 'checkmate,'" he cried, "you scoundrel!" Dalqak controlled himself and only said, "Mercy!"

Then the Prince commanded him to play again.

He obeyed, trembling like a naked man in bitter cold.

The Prince lost the second game too, but when the moment arrived to say 'Checkmate!'

Dalqak jumped up, ran into a corner, and hastily flung six rugs over himself.

There he lay hidden beneath six rugs and several cushions in order to escape the Prince's blows.

"Hey!" said the Prince, "what are you doing? What is this?" "Checkmate! Checkmate! Checkmate!" he replied, "O noble Prince."

[1] Book V, *v.* 3507.

XXV

THE INFANT MOHAMMED AND THE IDOLS[1]

I WILL tell you the story of Halīma's mystic experience,[2] that her tale may clear away your trouble.

When she parted Mustafā[3] from her milk, she took him up on the palm of her hand as though he were sweet basil and roses.

Fearing for the safety of her precious charge, she went towards the Ka'ba and entered the Hatīm.[4]

From the air she heard a voice saying, "O Hatīm, an exceedingly mighty Sun hath shone upon thee.

O Hatīm, to-day there marches into thee with pomp a glorious King, whose harbinger is Fortune.

O Hatīm, to-day thou wilt surely become anew the abode of exalted spirits.

[1] Book IV, *v.* 915.
[2] Halīma, a Bedouin woman, is said to have been Mohammed's nurse and foster-mother.
[3] Mohammed.
[4] The name Hatīm is properly given to a semi-circular wall adjoining the north and west corners of the Ka'ba. Here it denotes the space between the wall and the Ka'ba.

The spirits of the holy will come to thee from every quarter in troops and multitudes, drunken with desire."

Halīma was bewildered by that voice, for neither in front nor behind was anyone to be seen.

She laid Mustafā on the earth, that she might search after the sweet sound;

Then she cast her eyes to and fro, saying, "Where is that kingly crier of mysteries?"

Seeing no one, she became distraught and despairing: her body trembled like a willow-bough.

She returned towards that righteous Child, but could not see Mustafā where she had left him.

Amazement fell upon her heart: a great darkness of grief encompassed her.

She ran to the dwellings hard by, crying, "Alas, who has carried off my single Pearl?"

The Meccans said, "We have no knowledge: we knew not that a child was there."

She shed so many tears and made such a lamentation that all began to weep for her.

Beating her breast, she sobbed so mightily that the stars were made to sob by her sobbing.

An old man with a staff approached her, saying, "Why, what hath befallen thee, O Halīma?"

She replied, "I am Mohammed's trusted foster-mother: I was taking him back to his grand-sire.

When I arrived in the Hatīm, I heard voices from the air and laid the Child down,

To see whence the sounds came that were so melodious and beautiful.

I saw no sign of anyone about, yet the voices never ceased for a moment.

I was lost in bewilderment. On coming to my-self, I could not see the Child. Oh, the sorrow of my heart!"

"Daughter," said the old man, "do not grieve. I will show unto thee a Queen,

Who, if she wish, will tell thee what has hap-pened to the Child: she knows where he went and where he is now."

He brought her to 'Uzzā,[1] saying, "This Idol is greatly prized for information concerning the Unseen.

Through her we have found thousands who were lost, when we betook ourselves to her in devotion."

Then he bowed low before her and said, "O Sovereign of the Arabs, O Sea of munifi-cence,

Thou hast done many favours to us, O 'Uzzā, so that we have been delivered from snares.

[1] One of three goddesses whom the pre-Islamic Arabs worshipped as daughters of Allah.

In hope of thee this Halīma of the tribe Sa'd
hath come under the shadow of thy bounty,

For an infant child of hers is lost: the name of
the child is Mohammed."

When he pronounced the name "Mohammed"
all the Idols at once fell headlong and prostrate,

Saying, "Begone, old man! Why dost thou
inquire after this Mohammed by whom we
are deposed?

By him we are overthrown and reduced to a
heap of stones: by him we are made con-
temptible and worthless.

Avaunt, old man! Do not kindle mischief.
Hark, do not burn us in the flame of Mohammed's jealousy.

Avaunt, old man, for God's sake, lest thou too
be burnt in the fire of Fore-ordainment.

What squeezing of the dragon's tail is this?
Hast thou any inkling what the news of Mohammed's advent is?

At these tidings the heart of sea and mine will
surge; at these tidings the Seven Heavens
will tremble."

The old man's staff dropped from his hand;
his teeth chattered; like a naked man in
winter, he shuddered and cried, "Woe is me."

When Halīma saw him in such a state of terror,
self-control deserted her.

"Once before," she cried, "they of the Invisible
carried off my Child—they of the Invisible,
the green-winged ones of Heaven.

Of whom shall I complain? Whom shall I tell?
I am crazy and in a hundred minds.

His jealousy hath closed my lips, so that I cannot declare the mystery: I can only say, 'My
Child is lost.'

If I should say aught else now, the people would
bind me with chains as though I were mad."

The old man said to her, "O Halīma, rejoice;
bow down in thanksgiving, and do not rend
thy face.

Do not grieve: he will not be lost to thee; nay,
but the whole world will be lost in him.

Always, before and behind, he hath myriads of
zealous guardians watching over him.

Didst not thou see how the Idols, with all their
magic arts, fell headlong at the name of thy
Child?

This is a marvellous epoch on the earth: I am
grown old, but never have I witnessed aught
like this."

XXVI

THE SŪFĪS WHO SOLD THE
TRAVELLER'S ASS[1]

A SŪFĪ, after journeying, arrived at a monastery
for dervishes; he took his mount and led it
to the stable.

With his own hand he gave it a little water and
some fodder: he was not such a Sūfī as the
one we told of before.[2]

He took precautions against neglect and foolishness, but when the Divine destiny comes to
pass, of what avail is precaution?

The Sūfīs were poor and destitute: poverty
almost entails an infidelity that brings the
soul to perdition.

O thou rich man who art full-fed, beware of
mocking at the unrighteousness of the suffering poor.

On account of their destitution that Sūfī flock
adopted the expedient of selling the Ass,

Saying, "In case of necessity a carcase is lawful food: many a vicious act is made virtuous
by necessity."

[1] Book II, *v.* 514.
[2] See Story IV.

Having sold the little Ass, they fetched dainty viands and lit candles.

Jubilation arose in the monastery. "To-night," they cried, "there shall be dainties and music and dancing and voracity.

No more of this carrying the beggar's wallet, no more of this abstinence and three-days' fasting!"

The Traveller, tired by the long journey, rejoiced to see the favour with which they regarded him.

One by one they caressed him and played the game of bestowing pleasant attentions on him.

When he saw this, he said, "If I don't make merry to-night, when shall I have such good reasons for it again?"

They consumed the viands and began the *samā'* ;[1] the monastery was filled with smoke and dust up to the roof—

The smoke of the kitchen, the dust raised by the dancing feet, the tumult of soul aroused by longing and ecstasy.

Now, waving their hands, they would beat the floor with their feet; now, bowing low, they would sweep the dais with their foreheads.

Only after long waiting does the Sūfī gain his desire from Fortune; hence the Sūfī is a great eater;

Except, to be sure, the Sūfī who has eaten his

[1] The musical dance of Muslim dervishes.

fill of the Light of God: he is free from the shame of beggary;

But of these there are only a few amongst thousands; the rest live under the protection of his (the perfect Sūfī's) spiritual empire.

When the *samā'* had run its course from beginning to end, the minstrel struck up a deep-sounding strain.

He sang "The Ass is gone, the Ass is gone," and made the whole company sharers in the ditty.

Till daybreak they were dancing rapturously, clapping their hands and singing "The Ass is gone, the Ass is gone, my son!"

By way of imitation, that Sūfī began to sing in tones of impassioned feeling the same phrase, "The Ass is gone."

When the pleasure and excitement and music and dancing were over, day dawned and they all said farewell.

The monastery was deserted and the Sūfī remained alone: he set about shaking the dust from his baggage.

He brought out the baggage from his cell to pack it on the Ass, for he desired companions on his journey.

He made haste to join his fellow-travellers, but when he went into the stable he did not find the Ass.

"The servant," he said to himself, "has taken
it to water, because it drank little water last
night."

When the servant came the Sūfī asked, "Where
is the Ass?" "Look at your beard,"[1] he replied; and this started a quarrel.

The Sūfī said, "I entrusted the Ass to you. I
put you in charge of the Ass.

Discuss the matter reasonably, don't argue, but
deliver back to me what I delivered to you;

And if you obstinately refuse, then look here,
let us go for judgement to the Cadi!"

The servant said, "I was overpowered: the Sūfīs
rushed on me, and I was in fear of my life.

Do you throw a liver with the parts next it
amongst cats and then seek the traces of it?

One cake of bread amongst a hundred hungry
people, one starved cat before a hundred dogs?"

"I grant," said the Sūfī, "that they took the
Ass from you by violence, aiming at the life
of wretched me;

But you never came and said, 'They are taking
away your Ass, O dervish,'

So that I might have bought it back from the
purchaser, or else they might have divided
the money[2] amongst themselves.

----

[1] *i.e.* "don't ask childish questions."
[2] The money which the Sūfī would have paid as a ransom
for his Ass.

There were a hundred ways of mending the
  matter when they were present, but now each
  one is gone to a different clime.

Why didn't you come and say, 'O stranger, a
  terrible outrage has been committed'? "

"By God!" said he, "I came several times to
  inform you of these doings,

But you went on singing 'The Ass is gone, O
  son' with more gusto than all the others;

So I was always going away, saying to myself,
  'He is aware of it, he is satisfied with what
  God has decreed, he is a gnostic.' "

The Sūfī replied, "They all sang it so gleefully,
  and I too felt delight in singing it.

Blind imitation of them has brought me to ruin:
  a thousand curses on that imitation!"

XXVII

THE FOUR BEGGARS WHO WISHED TO BUY GRAPES[1]

A CERTAIN man gave a dirhem to four Beggars. One of them, a Persian, said, "I will spend it on *angūr*."

The second, who was an Arab, cried, "Nay, I want *'inab*, not *angūr*, you rascal!"

The third was a Turk: he said, "The money is mine: I don't want *'inab*, I want *uzum*."

The fourth, being a Greek, said, "Stop this talk: I want *istāfīl*."[2]

They began to fight because they were unaware of the meaning of the words.

In their folly they smote each other with their fists: they were full of ignorance and empty of knowledge.

This difference cannot be removed till a spiritual Solomon, skilled in tongues,[3] shall intervene.

O ye wrangling birds, hearken, like the falcon, to the falcon-drum of the King!

[1] Book II, *v.* 3681.

[2] σταφυλή.

[3] According to the *Qur'ān*, Solomon was acquainted with the speech of birds and animals.

93

Come now, from every quarter set out with
joy, flying away from diversity towards Oneness.

Wheresoever ye be, turn your faces towards it :[1]
this is the thing He hath not forbidden unto
you at any time.

[1] *Qur'ān*, II, 145.

XXVIII

MOSES AND THE SHEPHERD[1]

MOSES saw a shepherd on the way, who was
saying, "O God who choosest as Thou wilt,
Where art Thou, that I may become Thy ser-
vant and sew Thy shoes and comb Thy head?
That I may wash Thy clothes and kill Thy lice
and bring milk to Thee, O worshipful One;
That I may kiss Thy little hand and rub Thy little
feet and sweep Thy little room at bedtime."
On hearing these foolish words, Moses said,
"Man, to whom are you speaking!"
He answered, "To Him who created us and
brought this earth and heaven to sight."
"Hark!" said Moses, "you are a very wicked
man: indeed you are no true believer, you
have become an infidel.
What babble is this? What blasphemy and
raving? Stuff some cotton into your mouth!
The stench of your blasphemy hath made the
whole world stink: your blasphemy hath
torn the mantle of Religion to rags.
Shoes and socks are fitting for you, but how
are such things right for the Lord of glory?

[1] Book II, v. 1720.

Truly, the friendship of a fool is enmity:
the high God is not in want of suchlike
service."

The shepherd said, "O Moses, thou hast closed
my mouth and thou hast burned my soul
with contrition."

He rent his garment, heaved a sigh, turned in
haste towards the desert and went his way.

A Revelation came to Moses from God—"Thou
hast parted My servant from Me.

Wert thou sent as a prophet to unite, or wert
thou sent to sever?

I have bestowed on everyone a particular mode
of worship, I have given everyone a peculiar
form of expression.

In regard to him these words are praiseworthy,
in regard to thee blameworthy: honey for
him, poison for thee.

The idiom of Hindustān is excellent in the
Hindūs; the idiom of Sind is excellent in the
people of Sind.

I look not at tongue and speech, I look at the
spirit and the inward feeling.

I gaze into the heart to see whether it be lowly,
though the words uttered be not lowly.

Enough of phrases and conceptions and metaphors! I want burning, burning: become
familiar with that burning!

Light up a fire of love in thy soul, burn all
thought and expression away!
O Moses, they that know the conventions are
of one sort, they whose souls and spirits burn
are of another sort."

The Religion of Love is apart from all religions.
The lovers of God have no religion but God
alone.

XXIX

THE CAT AND THE MEAT[1]

THERE was a man, a householder, who had a
very sneering, sluttish, and rapacious wife.

She would devour everything he brought
home, and the poor man was reduced to
silence.

One day, having a guest, he brought home some
meat which had cost him infinite toil and
hardship.

His wife ate it up; she consumed all the *kabāb*[2]
and wine, and when her husband came in she
put him off with lies.

"Where is the meat?" he asked. "Our guest
has arrived: one must set nice food before a
guest."

"The cat has eaten it," said she; "go and buy
some more if possible."

He called his servant. "Fetch the scales, Aybak:
I will weigh the cat."

He found that the cat weighed half a maund.[3]
"O deceitful woman," he cried,

[1] Book V, *v.* 3409.
[2] Roast meat.
[3] The *man* (maund) is about two pounds avoirdupois.

98

"The meat was half a maund and six drachms over, and the cat is just half a maund, my lady!

If this is the cat, then where is the meat? or if this is the meat, where is the cat?"

XXX

HOW BĀYAZĪD PERFORMED THE PILGRIMAGE[1]

ON his way to the Ka'ba, Bāyazīd sought earnestly to meet the Khizr of the age.[2]

He espied an old man whose body was curved like the new moon; in him was the majesty and lofty speech of saints;

His eyes sightless, his heart radiant as the sun; like an elephant dreaming of Hindustān,

Beholding with closed eyes a hundred delights; when his eyes open, he sees naught thereof. How wonderful!

Many a wonder is made manifest in sleep: in sleep the heart becomes a window.

He that is awake and dreams fair dreams is the knower of God: smear your eyes with his dust!

Bāyazīd sat down before him and asked about

[1] Book II, v. 2231. Bāyazīd of Bistām was a famous Persian Sūfī of the ninth century.

[2] i.e. the supreme head of the hierarchy of saints. Khizr, sometimes identified with Elijah, is a mysterious personage who gained immortality by drinking of the Water of Life. The Sūfīs believe that he meets them in their wanderings, or appears in their visions, and imparts to them all sorts of esoteric lore.

his condition: he found him to be a dervish and also a family man.

"O Bāyazīd," said he, "whither art thou faring? To what place wouldst thou take the baggage of travel in a strange land?"

Bāyazīd answered, "I start for the Ka'ba at daybreak." "Eh," cried the other, "what hast thou as provision for the road?"

"Two hundred silver dirhems," said he. "Here they are, tied in the corner of my cloak."

He said, "Make a circuit seven times round me, and reckon this to be better than the circumambulation of the Ka'ba;

And lay the dirhems before me, O generous man. Know that thou hast made the Greater Pilgrimage[1] and won to thy desire,

And thou hast performed the Lesser Pilgrimage[2] too and gained the life everlasting, and thou hast run up the Hill of Purity[3] and been purged.

By the truth of the Truth which thy soul hath seen, I swear that He hath chosen me above His House.

Albeit the Ka'ba is the House of His worship, my form in which I was created is the House of His inmost mystery.

[1] *Hajj*.
[2] *'Umra*.
[3] The Hill *Safā*, which the pilgrims ascend after having performed the ceremony of circumambulation (*tawāf*).

Never since God made the Ka'ba hath He
entered it, and none but the Living God
hath ever entered into this House of mine.

When thou hast seen me thou hast seen God:
thou hast circled round the true Ka'ba.

To serve me is to obey and glorify God. Beware! Deem not that God is separate from
me.

Open thine eyes well and look on me, that thou
mayst behold the Light of God in man."

Bāyazīd gave heed to these mystic sayings and
put them as a golden ring in his ear.

XXXI

THE ARAB OF THE DESERT AND HIS DOG[1]

THE dog was dying, the Arab was shedding
 tears and crying, "Woe is me!"

A passing beggar asked him the cause of his tears,
 and for whom he was making such a lament.

He replied, "I owned a dog of excellent dis-
 position; look, he is dying on the road.

He hunted for me by day and kept watch at
 night; he was a sharp-eyed hunter and a
 driver away of thieves."

"What is the matter with him? Has he been
 wounded?" "No; the pangs of hunger have
 brought him to the last gasp."

"Show patience in this trouble and affliction:
 the grace of God bestows a recompense on
 those who suffer patiently."

Afterwards the beggar said to him, "O noble
 chief, what is inside this well-filled wallet in
 your hand?"

"Bread," said he, "and the remnants of last
 night's meal: I am taking them with me to
 nourish my body."

[1] Book V, *v.* 477.

103

"Why don't you give them to the dog?" "I have not love and charity to that extent. One cannot get bread on the road without spending money, but tears cost nothing."

"Dust on thy head," cried the beggar, "thou water-skin full of wind! To thee a crust of bread is more precious than tears."

XXXII

THE TEACHER WHO IMAGINED HE WAS ILL[1]

THE boys in a certain school, who suffered at the
    hands of their master from weariness and toil,
Consulted how they might stop his work and
    compel him to let them go.
One, the cleverest of them all, proposed that
    he should say, "Master, why are you so pale?
I hope you are well. You have lost your colour:
    is it the effect of bad air or of fever?"
He continued, "On hearing this he will begin
    to fancy that he is ill. Do you too, brother,
    help me in like manner.
When you come in through the school door
    say to him, 'Master, is your health good?'
Then that fancy of his will increase a little, for
    fancy can drive a sensible man mad.
After us, let the third boy and the fourth and
    fifth show the same sympathy and concern,
So that, when thirty boys in succession tell this
    story, it may settle down in his mind."
"Bravo!" cried the boys; "may your fortune rest
    on God's favour, O sagacious one!"

[1] Book III, v. 1522.

They agreed, in firm covenant, that no fellow
    should alter the words;

And then, lest any tell-tale should reveal the
    plot, he administered an oath to them all.

The counsel of that boy prevailed over his com-
    panions; his intellect was the leader of the
    flock.

There is the same difference in human minds
    as in the outward forms of those who are
    beloved.[1]

From this point of view Mohammed said that a
    man's excellence lies hidden in his tongue.[2]

Next day, thinking of nothing else, the boys
    came from their homes to the "shop,"

And stood outside, waiting for that resolute
    fellow to go in first,

Because he was the source of the plan: the head
    is always an Imām to the foot.

He went in and said to the master, "Salaam! I
    hope you are well: you look pale."

The master said, "I have no ailment. Go and sit
    down and don't talk nonsense, hey!"

He denied it, but the dust of vain imagination
    struck a little upon his mind.

---

[1] The poet's doctrine of the innate difference in human
intellects is opposed to that of the Mu'tazilites, who held
that men are originally equal in this respect and that all
diversities arise from learning and experience.

[2] *i.e.* until he speaks, no one can judge of his intelligence.

Another boy came in and said the like, which
    strengthened that imagination a little more;
And so on and so on, till at last he was exceed-
    ingly alarmed as to his state of health.
The master became unnerved; he sprang up
    and slowly made his way home,
Angry with his wife and saying, "Her love is
    weak: I am so ill, and she never asked or
    inquired;
She did not even inform me about my colour:
    she is ashamed of me and wishes to be free."
He came home and fiercely opened the door,
    the boys following at his heels.
His wife said, "Is it well with thee? How hast
    thou come so soon? May no evil happen to
    thy goodly person!"
He said, "Are you blind? Look at my colour
    and appearance; even strangers are lament-
    ing my affliction,
While you, within my house, from hatred and
    hypocrisy, do not see what anguish I am
    suffering."
"O Sir," said his wife, "there is nothing wrong
    with thee: 'tis only thy vain fancy and opinion."
He replied, "Will you still be wrangling, O
    harlot? Don't you see the change in my looks
    and how I tremble?
If you are blind and deaf, what fault of mine is
    it? I am in pain and grief and woe."

She said, "Sir, I will bring the mirror in order
that thou mayst know I am innocent."

"Begone," said he; "a plague on you and your
mirror! You are always engaged in hatred
and malice and sin.

Lay my bed at once, that I may lie down, for
my head is sore."

The wife lingered; he bawled at her, "Be quick,
odious creature! This is just like you!"

The old woman brought the bed-clothes and
spread them. She said to herself, "I can do
no more, though my heart is burning.

If I speak, he will suspect me; and if I say
nothing, the affair will become serious.

If I tell him he is not ill, he will imagine that I
have an evil design and am making arrange-
ments to be alone.

'She is getting me out of the house,' he will say;
'she is plotting some wickedness.' "

As soon as the bed was made the master threw
himself down, sighing and moaning continually,

While the boys sat round, reciting their lesson
with a hundred sorrows in secret,

Thinking, "We have done all this, and still we
are detained: it was a badly built plan and
we are bad builders."

The clever boy said, "O good fellows, recite the lesson and make your voices loud."

When they raised their voices he said, "Boys, the noise we are making will do the master harm.

His headache will increase: is it worth his while to suffer such pain for the sake of a few pence?"

The master said, "He is right. Go away! My headache is worse. Get out!"

They bowed and said, "O honoured Sir, may illness and danger be far from you!"

Then they bounded off to their homes, like birds in quest of grain.

Their mothers were angry with them and said, "A school-day and you at play!"

Each boy offered excuses, saying, "Stop, mother! This sin does not proceed from us and is not caused by our fault.

By the destiny of Heaven our master has become ill and sick and afflicted."

The mothers said, "It is a trick and a lie: ye invent a hundred lies in your greed for amusement.

To-morrow we will visit the master, that we may see what is at the bottom of this trick of yours."

"Go in God's name," said the boys, "and find out whether we are lying or telling the truth."

Next morning the mothers came and found the
    master in bed, like one who is gravely ill,

Perspiring under a great many coverlets, his
    head bandaged and his face enveloped in the
    quilt.

He was moaning softly. They all began to cry,
    "*Lā hawl.*"[1]

They said, "Master, may all be well! This
    headache—by thy soul, we were not aware of
    it."

"Neither was I," said he, "till these rascals
    called my attention to it.

I was teaching and too busy to take notice,
    though such a grave malady lurked within
    me."

[1] See p. 17, note 2.

XXXIII

THE UNSEEN ELEPHANT[1]

THE Elephant was in a dark house: some Hindūs
    had brought it for exhibition.

As seeing it with the eye was impossible, every-
    one felt it in the dark with the palm of his
    hand.

The hand of one fell on its trunk: he said, "This
    creature is like a water-pipe."

Another touched its ear: to him it appeared
    like a fan.

Another handled its leg: he said, "I found the
    Elephant's shape to be like a pillar."

Another laid his hand on its back: he said,
    "Truly this Elephant resembles a throne."

Had there been a candle in each one's hand, the
    difference would have gone out of their words.

[1] Book III, v. 1259. Religions are many, but God is One.
The intellect, groping in the dark, cannot form any true
conception of His nature. Only the clairvoyant eye of the
mystic sees Him as he really is.

XXXIV

PHARAOH AND HIS MAGICIANS[1]

WHEN Moses had returned home, Pharaoh
called his advisers and counsellors to his
presence.

They deemed it right that the King and Ruler
of Egypt should assemble the magicians from
all parts of Egypt.

Thereupon he sent many men in every direction
to collect the sorcerers.

In whatsoever region there was a renowned
magician, he sent flying towards him ten
active couriers.

There were two youths, famous magicians:
their magic penetrated into the heart of the
moon.

They milked the moon publicly and openly; in
their journeys they went mounted on a wine-
jar.

They caused the moonshine to seem like a piece
of linen; they measured and sold it speedily

And took the silver away: the purchaser, on
becoming aware of the fraud, would smite his
hand upon his cheeks in grief.

[1] Book III, v. 1157.

They invented a hundred thousand such tricks
of sorcery and did not follow behind, like
the rhyme-letter.[1]

When the King's message reached them, to
this effect: "The King desires your aid,

Because two dervishes[2] have come and marched
against the King and his palace.

They have naught with them except a rod,
which becomes a dragon at his command.

The King and the whole army are helpless: all
have been brought to lamentation by these
twain.

A remedy must be sought in magic, that maybe
ye will save their lives from these enchan-
ters"—

When the King's courier gave the message to
the two young magicians, a great fear and
love descended on the hearts of them both.

The vein of spiritual affinity began to throb,[3]
and in amazement they laid their heads upon
their knees.

Inasmuch as the knee is the Sūfī's school,[4] the
two knees are sorcerers for solving a difficulty.

[1] *i.e.* they did not imitate others.
[2] Moses and Aaron.
[3] Because God had predestined them to have faith in
Moses and become his followers.
[4] Referring to the attitude of Sūfīs when engaged in holy
meditation.

*How those two magicians summoned their father
from the grave and questioned their father's spirit
concerning the real nature of Moses, on whom
be peace.*

Afterwards they said, "Come, O mother, where
is our father's grave? Do thou show us the
way."

She led them to his grave: there they kept a
three-days' fast for the sake of the King.

Then they said, "O father, the King in con-
sternation hath sent us a message

That two men have brought him to sore straits
and destroyed his prestige with the army.

There is not with them any weapons or soldiers;
nothing but a rod, and in the rod is a calamity
and bane.

Thou art gone into the world of the righteous,
though to outward seeming thou liest in a
tomb.

If that be magic, inform us; and if it be divine,
O spirit of our father,

In that case too inform us, so that we may bow
down before them and bring ourselves in
touch with an elixir.[1]

We are despairing, and a hope has come; we
are banished, and Mercy has drawn us back."

[1] The prophets and saints are often compared to the
Philosophers' Stone which transmutes base metal into pure
gold.

How the dead Magician answered his sons.

He cried, "O my dearest sons, it rests with God to declare this matter plainly.

It is not permitted to me to speak openly and freely, though the mystery is not far from mine eye;

But I will show unto you a sign, that this hidden thing may be made manifest to you.

O light of mine eyes, when ye go thither become acquainted with the place where he sleeps,

And at the time when that Sage is asleep make for the rod, abandon fear.

If thou art able to steal it, he is a magician: the means of dealing with a magician are present with thee;

But if thou canst not steal it, beware, beware! That man is of God, he is the messenger of the Almighty and is divinely guided.

Let Pharaoh occupy the world from east to west, he will fall headlong. God and then war![1]

I give thee this true sign, O soul of thy father, inscribe it in thy heart: God best knoweth the truth.

O soul of thy father, when a magician sleeps, there is none to direct his magic and craft.

---

[1] *i.e.* the idea of opposing God is absurd.

When the shepherd has gone to sleep, the wolf
  becomes unafraid; when he falls asleep, his
  work is done;
But what hope or way hath the wolf to reach
  the animal whose shepherd is God?
O soul of thy father, this is the decisive sign:
  even if a prophet die, God exalteth him."[1]

*Comparison of the sublime Qur'ān to the rod of
Moses, and the death of Mohammed, on whom
be peace, to the sleep of Moses, and those who
would alter the Qur'ān to the two young Magicians who attempted to carry off the rod of Moses
when they found him asleep.*

The lovingkindness of God made a promise to
  Mohammed, saying, "If thou shalt die, yet
  this Lesson[2] shall not die.
I will exalt thy Book and Miracle, I will defend
  the *Qur'ān* from those who would make it
  more or less.
I will exalt thee in both worlds, I will drive
  away the scoffers from thy Tidings.
None shall be able to add or omit therein. Do
  not thou seek a guardian better than Me.

[1] The conclusion of the Story may be summarised in a
few words. When the two Magicians approach Moses, the
Rod turns into a Dragon. They flee in panic, are stricken
with fever, and at the point of death entreat Moses to pardon
their presumption, acknowledging him to be the prophet of
God.
[2] The *Qur'ān*.

116

Day by day I will increase thy splendour; I
will strike thy name on gold and silver.

For thy sake I will prepare pulpit and prayer-
niche: in My love for thee thy vengeance
hath become My vengeance.

Thy followers, from fear, utter thy name
covertly and hide when they perform their
prayers;

From terror and dread of the accursed infidels
thy Religion is hidden underground;

But I will fill the world from end to end with
minarets; I will blind the eyes of the recalci-
trant.

Thy servants will occupy cities and seize power:
thy Religion will extend from the Fish to the
Moon.[1]

I will keep it living until the Resurrection: be
not thou afraid of the annulment of thy
Religion, O Mustafā!

O My Prophet, thou art not a sorcerer: thou art
truthful, thou wearest the mantle of Moses.

To thee the *Qur'ān* is even as the rod of Moses:
it swallows up infidelities like a dragon.

If thou sleepest beneath a sod, yet deem as his
rod My Word which thou hast spoken.

Assailants have no power over his rod. Sleep,
then, O King, a blessed sleep!

[1] The Earth was supposed by Muslim cosmogonists to
rest on the back of a Fish floating in a great Ocean.

Whilst thy body is asleep in the tomb, thy Light in Heaven[1] hath strung a bow for thy war against the infidels.

The philosopher and that which his mouth doeth—the bow of thy Light is piercing them with arrows."

Thus He did, and even more than He said. The Prophet slept, but his fortune and prosperity slumbered not.

[1] The pre-existent form of Mohammed, which is the first thing that God created, was conceived as a celestial Light: this Light (*Nūr Muhammadī*) became incarnate in Adam and in the whole series of prophets after him from generation to generation until its final appearance in the historical Mohammed himself. According to the Shī'ites, however, it passed from Mohammed to 'Alī and the Imāms of his House, while the Sūfī saints also claim to be its torch-bearers.

XXXV

THE MOST BEAUTIFUL CITY[1]

A LOVED one said to her lover, "O youth, thou
hast seen many cities abroad.

Which of them, then, is the fairest?" He replied, "The city where my sweetheart dwells."

Wherever the carpet is spread for our King 'tis
a spacious plain though it be narrow as the
eye of a needle.

Wherever there is a Joseph beautiful as the
moon, 'tis Paradise, even if it be the bottom
of a well.

[1] Book III, v. 3808.

XXXVI

THE PATIENCE OF LUQMĀN[1]

LUQMĀN went to David, the pure of heart, and
    observed that he was making rings of iron,

And that the exalted King was casting the rings
    into each other.[2]

He had not seen the armourer's handicraft be-
    fore: he was astonished, and his curiosity
    increased—

"What can this be? I will ask him what he is
    making with the interwoven rings."

Again he said to himself, "Patience is better:
    patience is the quickest guide to the object
    of one's search."

When you ask no questions, the sooner will the
    secret be disclosed to you: the bird, patience,
    flies faster than all others;

And if you ask, the more slowly will your object
    be gained: what is easy will be made difficult
    by your impatience.

When Luqmān kept silence, straightway the
    ring-making was finished by David's crafts-
    manship.

[1] Book III, v. 1842.

[2] God taught David the art of making coats of mail
(*Qur'ān*, xxi, 80).

Then he fashioned a coat of mail and put it on in the presence of the noble and patient Luqmān.

"This," he said, "is an excellent garment, O young man, for warding off blows on the battlefield."

Luqmān said, "Patience too is of good effect, for it is the protection and defence against pain everywhere."

XXXVII

HOW JESUS FLED FROM THE FOOLS[1]

Jesus, son of Mary, was fleeing to a mountain:
you would say that a lion wished to shed his
blood.

A certain man ran after him and said, "Is it
well? There is none pursuing thee: why art
thou fleeing like a bird?"

But Jesus still ran on so quickly that on account
of his haste he did not answer him.

The man went in pursuit of Jesus for the distance of one or two fields; then he invoked
Jesus with the utmost earnestness,

Saying, "For God's sake, stop one moment! I
have a difficulty concerning thy flight.

From whom art thou fleeing, O noble one? No
lion is chasing thee, no enemy, and there is
no fear or danger."

He said, "I am fleeing from the fool. Begone! I am saving myself. Do not hinder
me!"

"Why," said he, "art not thou the Messiah by
whom the blind and deaf are restored to
sight and hearing?"

[1] Book III, *v.* 2570.

He said, "Yea." Said the other, "Art not thou
the King in whom the spells of the Unseen
World have their abode,

So that, when thou chantest them over a dead
man, he springs up like a lion that has caught
his prey?"

He said, "Yea, I am he." Said the other, "Dost
not thou make living birds out of clay,[1] O
beauteous one?"

He said, "Yea." Said the other, "Then, O pure
Spirit, thou doest whatsoever thou wilt: of
whom hast thou fear?

With such miraculous evidence, who in the
world would not be a slave devoted to
thee?"

Jesus said, "By the holy Essence of God, the
Maker of the body and the Creator of the
soul in eternity;

By the sanctity of the pure Essence and Attributes of Him for whose sake the collar of
Heaven is rent,

I swear that the spells and the Most Great
Name which I pronounced over the deaf and
blind were good in their effects.

I pronounced them over the stony mountain:
it was cloven and tore upon itself its mantle
down to the navel.

I pronounced them over the corpse: it came to

[1] *Qur'ān*, III, 43.

life. I pronounced them over nonentity: it became entity.

I pronounced them lovingly over the heart of the fool hundreds of thousands of times, and 'twas no cure for his folly."

XXXVIII

THE MAN WHO THOUGHT HE HAD PRAYED TO GOD IN VAIN[1]

ONE night a certain man was crying "Allah!" till his lips grew sweet with praise of Him.

The Devil said, "Prithee, O garrulous one, where is the response 'Here am I' to all this 'Allah'?

Not a single response is coming from the Throne: how long will you cry 'Allah' with grim face?"

He became broken-hearted and lay down to sleep: in a dream he saw Khadir[2] amidst the verdure,

Who said, "Hark, you have held back from praising God: why do you repent of having called unto Him?"

He replied, "No 'Here am I' is coming to me in response, hence I fear that I am turned away from the Door."

Said Khadir, "Nay; God saith, 'That 'Allah' of thine is My 'Here am I,' and that suppli-

---

[1] Book III, v. 189.
[2] For Khadir or Khizr, see p. 100, note 2.

cation and grief and ardour of thine is My
messenger to thee.

Thy fear and love are the noose to catch My
favour: beneath every 'O Lord' of thine is
many a 'Here am I' from Me.'"

XXXIX

THE HOUSE BUILT ON HYPOTHESES[1]

A HOMELESS man was hastily seeking a house.
One of his friends took him to a house in
ruins

And remarked, "If it had a roof, it would do
for you to live in, and you would be almost
next door to me.

Your family too would be comfortable, if there
were another room in it."

"Yes," he replied, "it is nice to live beside
friends but, my dear soul, one cannot lodge
in IF."

[1] Book II, *v.* 739.

XL

SULTĀN MUHAMMAD KHWĀRAZMSHĀH
AND THE PEOPLE OF SABZAWĀR[1]

MUHAMMAD Alp Ulugh Khwārazmshāh marched
against Sabzawār, which was a city of refuge
for all rascals.[2]

When his troops had reduced it and were about
to massacre the foe,

They threw themselves at his feet, crying,
"Mercy! Make us thralls, only spare our
lives.

Whatsoever tax and tribute thou mayst demand,
we will pay that and more to thee at every
season.

O lion-hearted King, our lives are thine, but
leave them in trust with us for a little while."

He replied, "Ye shall not save your lives from
me unless ye bring an Abū Bakr into my
presence.[3]

[1] Book V, *v.* 845. Sultān Muhammad Khwārazmshāh
(1199-1220 A.D.) ruled over a great empire in Central Asia.
He fled before the Mongols and died in exile. Sabzawār
was situated in the Bayhaq district to the west of Nīshāpūr.

[2] Most of its population were fanatical Shī'ites.

[3] Any person bearing the name of the first orthodox
Caliph would be anathema in such a hotbed of heresy.

Unless ye bring someone whose name is Abū
  Bakr as a gift to me from your city, O mis-
  creants,
I will mow you down like corn, ye vile people!
  I will accept neither tribute nor fair words."
They offered him many sacks of gold, saying,
  "Do not demand an Abū Bakr from a city
  like this.
How should there be an Abū Bakr in Sabzawār,
  or a dry clod at the bottom of the river?"
The King averted his face from the gold and
  said, "O infidels, unless ye present me with
  an Abū Bakr,
'Tis of no avail. I am not a child, that I should
  stand dumbfounded at the sight of gold and
  silver."
O base wretch, until thou prostrate thyself in
  prayer thou wilt not be saved, even if thou
  shouldst traverse the whole mosque on thy
  séant.[1]

They despatched emissaries, right and left, to
  search for an Abū Bakr in this God-forsaken
  place,
And after three days and nights spent in hurrying to and fro an emaciated man of that name
  was discovered.
He was a wayfarer, who had fallen ill: they

[1] This verse is a comment by the poet.

found him lying at the point of death in a corner of a ruined house.

"Rise up!" they cried; "the Sultān hath summoned thee. Thou wilt be the means of saving our people from massacre."

He answered, "If my feet could carry me, I would have gone on to my destination.

How should I have remained in this abode of my enemies? I would have journeyed towards the city of my friends."

They brought a bier and lifted upon it the Abū Bakr whom I celebrate,

And the bearers set off to convey him to Khwārazmshāh, in order that the King might behold the sign.

Sabzawār is this world, where the man of God is abandoned and left to perish.

Khwārazmshāh is God Almighty, who demands of this unrighteous people the gift of a pure heart.

XLI

THE MAN WHO WISHED TO LEARN THE LANGUAGE OF BEASTS AND BIRDS[1]

A YOUNG man said to Moses, "Teach me the
　　language of the animals,
That perchance from the voice of animals and
　　wild beasts I may get a lesson concerning my
　　religion.
Since the languages of the children of Adam
　　are entirely for the sake of acquiring wealth
　　and reputation,
It may be that the animals have a different care
　　—namely, to meditate on the hour of passing
　　away from the world."
"Begone," said Moses; "abandon this vain
　　desire, for it is fraught with much danger
　　before and behind.
Seek the religious lesson and the gift of spiritual
　　wakefulness from God, not from books and
　　words and lips."
He answered, "O generous one, 'tis unworthy
　　of thy bounty to disappoint me of the object
　　of my desire.

[1] Book III, v. 3266.

Thou art the vicegerent of God: if thou prevent me, I shall be in despair."

Moses said, "O Lord, surely the accursed Devil has taken possession of this simple man.

If I teach him, it will be harmful to him; and if I refuse to teach him, he will lose heart."

God said, "Teach him, O Moses, for We in our lovingkindness never reject anyone's prayer.

Grant his wish: let him have a free hand to choose good or evil."

Once more did Moses warn him kindly, saying, "The thing thou desirest will make thy face pale.

Give up this idle passion, fear God! The Devil hath instructed thee for his own cunning purposes."

He replied, "At any rate, teach me the language of the dog at the door and the feathered domestic fowl."

"Hark," said Moses, "thou knowest best! Go, thy wish is granted: the language of both will be revealed to thee."

At daybreak, in order to make trial, he stood waiting on the threshold.

The maid-servant shook the table-cloth; a

piece of bread, the remains of last night's supper, fell out.

A Cock snatched it up, as though it were the stake in a race. The Dog cried, "You have defrauded me.

You can eat corn and barley and other grains, while I cannot, O jubilant one.

And now you deprive the dogs of this little crust of bread, the bread which belongs to us!"

"Hush!" said the Cock, "do not grieve. God will give you something else instead of this.

The Master's horse is about to die: to-morrow eat your fill and be happy.

The horse's death will be a feast-day for the dogs: you will get plenty of food without toil or trouble."

On hearing this speech, the man sold his horse. The Cock was disgraced in the eyes of the Dog.

Next day the Cock carried off the bread as before, and the Dog opened his mouth at him,

Saying, "O deceitful Cock, how long will you tell such lies? You are unrighteous and false and ignoble.

Where is the horse that you said would die? You are like a blind astrologer, your predictions are devoid of truth."

That knowing Cock answered, "His horse died in another place.

He sold the horse and escaped from loss: he cast the loss upon others;

But to-morrow his mule will die, and that will be good luck for the dogs. Say no more."

The covetous man immediately sold the mule and delivered himself from grief and loss.

On the third day the Dog addressed the Cock— "O prince of liars with your drums and kettle-drums!"

"Yes," said the Cock, "he sold the mule in haste; but to-morrow his slave will be stricken down,

And when his slave dies, the next of kin will scatter pieces of bread upon the dogs and beggars."

The Master heard this and sold his slave: he was saved from loss, he beamed with joy.

Next day the disappointed Dog said, "O drivelling Cock, where are all those good things you promised me?

How long, pray, will your falsehood and deceit continue? Verily, nothing but falsehood flies out of your nest."

The Cock answered, "Far be it from me and

from my kind that we should be afflicted
with falsehood.

We cocks are veracious like the muezzin: we
are observers of the sun and seekers of the
right time.

Though you clap us under an inverted bowl,
we still watch the sun inwardly.

To-morrow the Master himself will certainly die:
his heir will slaughter a cow for the funeral.

High and low will get pieces of bread and
dainties and viands in the midst of the
street."

When the man heard these things, he ran in hot
haste to the door of Moses, with whom God
conversed,

Rubbing his face in the dust from fear, and
crying, " Save me from this doom, O Kalīm!"[1]

Moses said to him, "Go, sell thyself and escape!
Since thou art so clever in avoiding loss, jump
out of the pit of death!

Throw the loss upon true believers! Make thy
purses and scrips double in size!

I beheld in the brick this destiny which to thee
became visible only in the mirror.

The intelligent foresee the end at the beginning,
the foolish see it only at the end."

[1] Moses is called Kalīmu'llāh, because God spoke to him
(*kallamahu*) on Mount Sinai.

Once more he made lamentation, saying, "O bounteous one, do not beat me on the head, do not rub into my face the sin I have committed."

Moses replied, "An arrow sped from the Archer's thumbstall, my lad; 'tis not the rule that it should turn back;

But I will crave of God's good dispensation that thou mayst take the Faith with thee at that hour.

When thou hast taken the Faith with thee, thou art living: when thou goest with the Faith thou art enduring for ever."

At the same instant the Master became indisposed: he felt qualms and they brought the basin.

'Tis the qualms of death, not indigestion: how should vomiting avail thee, O foolish ill-fortuned man?

Four persons carried him home: one of his legs was pressed on the other.[1]

At dawn Moses began his orison, crying, "O God, do not take the Faith away from him!

Act in royal fashion, forgive him, though he has sinned and behaved with impudence and transgressed exceedingly."

[1] In the death-agony. Cf. *Qur'ān*, lxxv, 29.

God answered, "Yes, I bestow the Faith upon him, and if thou wish I will bring him to life at this moment.

Nay, at this moment I will bring to life all the dead in the earth for thy sake."

XLII

THE FRIEND WHO SAID "I"[1]

A CERTAIN man knocked at his friend's door:
his friend asked, "Who is there?"

He answered, "I." "Begone," said his friend,
" 'tis too soon: at my table there is no place
for the raw."

How shall the raw one be cooked but in the
fire of absence? What else will deliver him
from hypocrisy?

He turned sorrowfully away, and for a whole
year the flames of separation consumed him;

Then he came back and again paced to and fro
beside the house of his friend.

He knocked at the door with a hundred fears
and reverences, lest any disrespectful word
might escape from his lips.

"Who is there?" cried his friend. He answered,
"Thou, O charmer of all hearts!"

"Now," said the friend, "since thou art I, come
in: there is no room for two I's in this house."

[1] Book I, *v.* 3056.

XLIII

THE PEOPLE OF SABĀ[1]

I AM reminded of the story of the people of
Sabā—how their balmy zephyr (sabā) was
turned into pestilence (wabā) by the words
of the foolish.[2]

That kingdom of Sabā resembles the great
big city which you may hear of from children
in their tales.

The children relate tales, but in their tales is
enfolded many a mystery and moral.

Though they tell many ridiculous things, yet
do thou ever seek the treasure that is hidden
in ruins.

Once there was a City very huge and great,[3]
but its size was the size of a saucer, no more
than that.

It was very huge and very broad and very long,
ever so big, as big as an onion.

[1] Book III, v. 2600. Sabā is the Sheba of the Bible.

[2] The Story of the Sabæans—their frowardness, their ingratitude for the blessings which they enjoyed, and their
consequent destruction—is related in Book III, v. 282 foll.

[3] This is "the children's tale." The "City" signifies the
Nature of Man, the microcosm in which the macrocosm is
contained.

The people of ten cities were assembled within it, but the whole amounted to three fellows with unwashed faces.

Within it were numberless people and folk, but the whole of them amounted to three beggarly fools.

One was very far-sighted and blind—blind to Solomon and seeing the leg of the ant;[1]

And the second was very sharp of hearing and exceedingly deaf—a treasure in which there is not a barley-corn's weight of gold;

And the third was naked and bare and indecent, but the skirts of his raiment were long.

The blind man said, "Look, an army is approaching: I see what people they are and how many."

The deaf man said, "Yes; I hear their voices and know what they are saying openly and secretly."

The naked man said, "I am afraid they will cut off something from the length of my skirt."

The blind man said, "Look, they have come

[1] Referring to the ant which said (*Qur'ān*, xxvii, 18), "*O ants, go into your dwellings, lest Solomon and his hosts crush you unawares.*"

near! Arise and let us flee before we suffer blows and chains."

"Yes," said the deaf man, "the noise is getting nearer. Come on, my friends!"

The naked man said, "Alas, they will covet my skirt and cut it off, and I have no protection."

All three left the City and came forth and in their flight entered a Village.[1]

In that Village they found a fat fowl, but not a mite of flesh on it; 'twas pitiful—

A dried-up dead fowl, and its bones had been pecked by crows till they were bare like threads.

They ate thereof as a lion eats of his prey; each of them became surfeited, like an elephant, with eating it.

All three ate thereof and grew mightily fat; they became like three very great and huge elephants,

So that each young man, because of his fatness, was too big to be contained in the world.

Notwithstanding such bigness and seven stout limbs,[2] they sprang forth through a chink in the door and departed.

---

[1] The world.
[2] The seven members of the body: head, breast, belly, arms and legs.

The way of creaturely death is an invisible way,
it comes not into sight; 'tis a marvellous
place of exit.

Lo, the caravans follow one after another
through this chink which is hidden from view
in the door.

If you look for that chink, you will not find it;
it is extremely unapparent, though there are
so many processions through it.

*Explaining what is signified by the far-sighted
blind man, the deaf man who is sharp of
hearing, and the naked man with the long
skirts.*

Know that Hope is the deaf man who has
often heard of our dying but has never
heard of his own death or regarded his own
decease.

The blind man is Greed: he sees the faults of
others, hair by hair, and tells them from
street to street,

But his blind eyes do not perceive one
mote of his own faults, albeit he is a fault-
finder.

The naked man is afraid that his skirt will be
cut off: how shall anyone cut off the skirt of
a naked man?

He is the Worldling, destitute and terrified: he

possesses nothing, yet he has dread of thieves.

Bare he came and naked he goes, and all the while his heart is bleeding with anguish on account of the thief.

XLIV

IBRĀHĪM SON OF ADHAM[1]

RECLINING on a throne, that renowned King
  heard at night a noise of tramping and shrill
  cries from the roof.

He heard loud footfalls on the roof of the
  palace and said to himself, "Who dares do
  this?"

He shouted from the window, "Who goes there?
  Methinks, 'tis no man, but a spirit."

A wondrous folk put their heads down from the
  roof, saying, "We are going round by night
  for the purpose of search."

"Eh, what are ye seeking?" "Camels," said
  they. He cried, "Take heed! Whoever sought
  a camel on a roof?"

They answered, "Why, then, art thou seeking
  God on the throne of empire?"

That was all. None saw him again: he vanished
  like a spirit from the sight of man.

[1] Book IV, v. 829. Ibrāhīm, son of Adham, of Balkh, a
celebrated ascetic and mystic, lived in the eighth century.
His legend, modelled upon the story of Buddha, makes him
a prince who abandoned his kingdom in order to devote
himself to God.

Although he was in their presence, his real self remained hidden from them: how should people see aught but the beard and dervish-cloak?

XLV

THE MAN WHO PRAYED THAT HE MIGHT RECEIVE HIS LIVELIHOOD WITHOUT LABOUR[1]

In the time of the prophet David a certain man,
  before sage and simple alike,
Used always to utter this prayer: "O God,
  bestow on me riches without trouble!
For Thou hast created me a lazybones, a re-
  ceiver of blows, a slow mover, a sluggard,
And one cannot lay upon sore-backed luckless
  donkeys the load carried by horses and mules.
I am lazy and asleep in this world of phenomenal
  being: I sleep in the shade of Thy bounty
  and munificence.
Surely for them that are lazily sleeping in the
  shade Thou hast ordained a livelihood in
  another fashion.
I crave the daily bread that comes without effort
  on my part, for I have no work except prayer."
Thus was he praying for a long while, all day
  until night and all night until morning.
The people laughed at his words, at the folly
  of his hope, and at his importunity:

[1] Book III, *v.* 1450.

146

"Marvellous! What is he saying—this idiot?
Or has somebody given him beng, which produces dementia?

The way to get daily bread is work and toil and
fatigue; God has bestowed on everyone a
handicraft and the power to seek his livelihood.

At present the King and Ruler and Messenger
of God is the prophet David, endowed with
many accomplishments.

Notwithstanding all his glory and majesty,
forasmuch as the favours of the Friend have
chosen him out,

His livelihood does not come to him without
his weaving coats of mail and labouring as a
craftsman.[1]

Now a God-forsaken abandoned wretch like this,
a low scoundrel and outcast from Heaven,

A backslider of this sort desires, without trading,
at once to fill his pockets with gain!"

One would say to him derisively, "Go and get
it! Thy daily bread has arrived, the messenger has brought the good news";

And another would laugh, saying, "Let us
have a share in the gift, O headman of the
village!"

All this abuse and ridicule could not induce
him to desist from his petitioning,

[1] See p. 120, note 2.

147

So that he became celebrated in the town as
one who looks for cheese in an empty wallet.

One morning, as he was praying with moans
and sighs, suddenly a cow ran into his house.

She butted with her horns, broke the bolt, and
jumped into the house; he sprang up and
bound her legs.

Then he cut her throat without delay, without
consideration, and without mercy,

And went to the butcher, in order that he might
rip off her hide forthwith.

The owner of the cow espied him and said,
"Hey, why did you kill my cow? Fool!
Brigand! Deal fairly with me."

He said, "God answered my ancient prayer.
The cow was my portion of daily bread: I
killed her. That is my reply."

The enraged owner seized him by the collar,
struck him in the face with his fist several
times,

And led him to the prophet David, saying,
"Come, you crazy fool and criminal!

What are you saying? What is this prayer of
yours? Don't laugh at my head and beard
and your own too, O rascal!

Hey, gather round, O Muslims! For God's
sake, how should his prayer make my property
belong to him?"

The people said, "He speaks truth, and this
prayer-monger seeks to act unjustly.

How should such a prayer be the means of acquiring property? Give back the cow or go
to prison!"

Meanwhile the poor man was turning his face
to Heaven and crying, "None knoweth my
spiritual experience save Thee.

Thou didst put the prayer into my heart, Thou
didst raise a hundred hopes in my heart.

Not idly was I uttering the prayer: like Joseph,
I had dreamed dreams."

When the prophet David came forth, he asked,
"What is all this about? What is the
matter?"

The plaintiff said, "O prophet of God, give me
justice. My cow strayed into his house.

He killed my cow. Ask him why he killed my
cow and bid him explain what happened."

David said to the poor man, "Speak! Why did
you destroy the property of this honourable
person?"

He replied, "O David, for seven years I was
engaged, day and night, in supplication and
entreaty,

Praying to God that He would give me a lawful
means of livelihood without trouble on my
part.

After all this calling and crying, suddenly I saw a cow in my house.

My eyes became dim, not on account of the food, but for joy that my supplication had been accepted.

I killed her that I might give alms, in thankfulness that He who knoweth things unseen had hearkened to my prayer."

David said, "Wipe out these words and set forth a legal plea in the dispute.

Who gave you the cow? Did you buy or inherit her? Will you take the crop when you are not the farmer?

You must pay this Muslim his money. Go, try to borrow it, and don't seek to do wrong."

"O King," said the poor man, "thou art telling me the same thing as my oppressors."

Then, prostrating himself, he cried, "O Thou who knowest the ardent faith within me, cast that flame into the heart of David;

Put in his heart that which Thou hast secretly let fall into mine, O Benefactor!"

He said this and began to weep and wail so that David was moved exceedingly.

David said to the plaintiff, "Give me a respite to-day. I will go to a solitary place and commune with God."

He shut the door, and then went quickly to the

prayer-niche and betook himself to the invocation that God answereth.

God revealed all to him, and he saw who was the man deserving of punishment.

Next day, when the litigants assembled and formed ranks before David, the plaintiff lifted up his voice in reproach.

David said to him, "Be silent! Go, abandon your claim, acquit this true believer of responsibility.

Seeing that God has thrown a veil over you, depart in silence and render due thanks unto God for what He has concealed."

He cried, "Oh, woe is me! What wisdom is this, what justice? Wilt thou establish a new law in my case?

Such wrong has never been done even to blind dogs; mountains and rocks are burst asunder by this iniquity."

Then said David, "O contumacious man, give him on the spot all that you possess.

Since 'twas not your fortune to be saved, little by little your wickedness has come to light.

Begone! Your wife and children have now become his slaves. Say no more!"

The plaintiff ran up and down in a frenzy, dashing stones against his breast with both hands,

While the people too began to blame David, for they were ignorant of the hidden circumstances.

The currish mob, which slays the oppressed and worships the oppressor, sprang forth from ambush and rushed towards David,

Crying, "O chosen prophet, this is unworthy of thee, 'tis manifest injustice; thou hast abased an innocent man for naught."

He said, "My friends, the time is come for his hidden secret to be displayed.

Arise, all of you, let us set out, that we may become acquainted with his mystery.

In such and such a plain there is a huge tree, its boughs thick and numerous and curved.

Its tent and tent-pegs are very firm; from its roots the smell of blood is coming to me.

Murder was done at the foot of that goodly tree: this ill-fated man killed his master.

The crime, which God's mercy concealed till now, has at last been brought to light through the ingratitude of this scoundrel,

Who never once looked upon his master's family, not even at Nawrūz[1] and other seasons of festival,

And never searched after the destitute children to relieve their want, or bethought him of the obligations he had received,

[1] The Persian New Year's Day.

And so proceeded, till for the sake of a cow this
accursed wretch is now felling his master's
son to the earth.

He himself has lifted the veil from his crime;
else God would have kept it hidden.

Wrong is covered up in the depths of the heart:
the wrong-doer exposes it to men,

Saying, 'Behold me! I have horns! Behold the
cow of Hell[1] in full view'! "

When they arrived at the tree, David said, "Tie
his hands fast behind him,

That I may bring his sin to light and plant the
banner of justice on the field.

O dog," said he, "you killed this man's father.
You were a slave; by murder you became a
lord.

You killed your master and seized his property:
God hath made it manifest.

Your wife was his handmaid: she has acted
unjustly towards her master.

The children she bore to him, male and female
—all of them from beginning to end are the
property of the master's heir.

You are a slave: your goods are his property.
You have demanded the Law: take the Law
and go: 'tis well.

[1] The fleshly soul, as is explained in the concluding verses
of the Story.

You killed your master miserably, whilst he was crying for mercy on this very spot,

And hastily hid the knife under the soil because of the terrible apparition which you beheld.

On the knife, too, the name of this hound is written who betrayed and murdered his master.

His head together with the knife is beneath! Dig ye back the soil, thus!"

Even so they did, and when they cleft the earth they found there the knife and the skull.

A tumult of lamentation went up from the people: everyone severed the girdle of unbelief.[1]

Then David said to him, "Come, O seeker of justice, and with that black face of yours receive the justice due to you!"

He ordered him to be killed in retaliation with the same knife: how should cunning deliver him from the knowledge of God?

Kill thy fleshly soul and make the world spiritually alive. She hath killed her master: make her thy slave.

The slayer of the cow is thy rational spirit: go, be not offended with the spirit that kills the flesh.

[1] Christians, Jews, and Zoroastrians wore a girdle (*zunnār*) to distinguish them from the Faithful.

The spirit is a captive, and craves of God daily bread won without toil, and bounty spread before it on a table.

Upon what does its daily bread depend? Upon its killing the cow, which is the origin of all evil.

XLVI

THE GHUZZ RAIDERS AND THE TWO NOTABLES[1]

THE murderous Ghuzz Turcomans raided a village. They found two notables and were about to put one of them to death.

When they had tied his hands, he said, "O princes and high pillars of the empire,

For what reason do ye seek to slay me? Wherefore, pray, are ye thirsting after my blood?

What is the sense, what is the object, in killing me, when I am so poor and destitute?"

One of the Ghuzz replied, "To strike awe into this friend of yours, so that he may produce his gold."

"Why," said the man, "he is poorer than I." "So he says," replied the Ghuzz, "but he has done it on purpose. He is rich."

"Since it is a matter of opinion," said the man, "he and I are in the same case: the probabilities are equal.

Kill him first, O princes, in order that I may be terrified and point out the way to the gold."

[1] Book II, *v.* 3046.

XLVII

HĀRŪT AND MĀRŪT[1]

LISTEN to the tale of Hārūt and Mārūt, O thou
to whose face we are devoted slaves.[2]

Hārūt and Mārūt were intoxicated with the
spectacle of God and the marvel of His
gradual temptation of them.

Such intoxication arises from His temptation:
you may judge, then, what intoxications are
wrought by the ascension to God?

If the bait in His snare produces intoxication
like this, what delights will the table of His
bounty reveal!

They were drunken and freed from the noose:
they were uttering rapturous cries in the
fashion of lovers;

But in their road there was an ambush and trial:

[1] Book III, *v.* 8oo. Hārūt and Mārūt were two angels, who
looked with contempt on the sinful state of men and received
permission to visit the earth, though God warned them of the
temptations to which they would be exposed. On coming
down to the earth, they fell in love with a beautiful woman
—Venus, according to some accounts—and seduced her.
Given the choice of punishment in this world or the next,
they preferred the former and were imprisoned in a pit at
Babylon.

[2] Husāmu'ddīn, to whom the *Mathnawī* is dedicated.

its mighty wind would sweep away mountains like a straw.

The Divine trial was driving them headlong;
but how should one who is drunken be conscious of these things?

To him pit and open field are one, to him dungeon and pit are a pleasant path to tread.

The mountain-goat runs up the high mountain
to feed in safety.

While browsing, suddenly he sees another trick
played by the ordinance of Heaven.

He casts his gaze upon another mountain, and
there he espies a she-goat.

Straightway his eyes are darkened: he leaps
madly from this mountain to that.

To him it seems as easy as to run round the
sink in the court of a house.

Those thousands of yards are made to appear to
him as two, in order that from mad infatua-
tion the impulse to leap may come to him.

As soon as he leaps, he falls midway between
the two pitiless mountains.

He had fled to the mountain to escape from the
hunters: his very refuge shed his blood.

Hārūt and Mārūt, being intoxicated with pride,
said, "Ah, we would rain upon the earth, like
clouds;

We would spread in this place of injustice a

carpet of justice and equity and devotion and faithfulness."

So they said; and the Divine Decree was saying to them, "Stop! Before your feet is many an unseen pitfall."

The Decree was saying this, but their ears were muffled in the veil of their hotheadedness.

All eyes and ears are shut, except in them that have escaped from themselves.

Who but Grace shall open the eyes? Who but Love shall allay the Wrath?

XLVIII

THE GRAMMARIAN AND THE BOATMAN[1]

A SELF-CONCEITED grammarian embarked in a
boat. Turning to the boatman, he asked,

"Have you ever studied grammar?" "No," he
replied. "Then," said the grammarian, "half
your life has been lost."

The boatman, heart-broken with grief, refrained
from answering him at the time.

The wind cast the boat into a whirlpool. The
boatman shouted to the grammarian,

"Tell me, can you swim?" "No," said he, "O
fair-spoken, well-favoured man."

"O grammarian," he cried, "your whole life
is lost, for the boat is sinking in this whirlpool."

Know that here *mahw* (self-naughting) is needed,
not *nahw* (grammar). If you are *mahw* (dead
to self), you may plunge into the sea without
peril.

The sea bears up one who is dead; but if

[1] Book I, *v.* 2835

he be living, how shall he escape from the sea?

When you have died to the fleshly nature, the sea of divine consciousness will raise you aloft.

XLIX

THE GARDENER AND THE THREE FRIENDS[1]

A GARDENER found in his orchard three men
who looked like thieves,

A Jurist and a Sharīf[2] and a Sūfī: each one an
impudent, knavish, perfidious rogue.

He said, "I have a hundred arguments against
these fellows, but they are united, and union
is strength.

I cannot cope singly with the three, so first I
will separate them, and when each is alone I
will tear out his moustache."

He employed a ruse to get the Sūfī away and
poison the minds of his friends against him.

"Go to the house," said he, "and fetch a rug
for your comrades."

Then he said to the two friends in private,
"Thou art a Jurist, and thy friend is a renowned Sharīf.

'Tis according to thy legal decision that we eat
our bread, 'tis by the wings of thy knowledge
that we fly;

[1] Book II, v. 2167.
[2] A descendant of the Prophet.

162

And thy friend is our prince and sovereign: he
  is a Sayyid of the Prophet's House.

Who is this gluttonous vile Sūfī that he should
  consort with noblemen like you?

When he comes back, beat him off and take
  possession of my orchard for a week.

My orchard? Nay, my life. Ye are dear to me
  as the apple of my right eye."

He tempted and beguiled them. Ah, one must
  not patiently submit to losing one's friend.

When they had driven the Sūfī away, the enemy
  went after him with a stout cudgel.

"O dog," he cried, "is it Sūfism that of a sudden
  you come into my orchard in spite of me?

Has Junayd[1] or Bāyazīd[2] directed you to behave
  so? From what Shaykh did you receive this
  instruction?"

Raising his cudgel, he belaboured the helpless
  Sūfī, cracked his head and half killed him.

"My score is paid," said the Sūfī, "but have a
  care for yourselves, O comrades!

Ye treated me as a foe. Look out! I am not
  more unfriendly than this scoundrel.

The cup which I have drunk ye must drink, and
  such a draught is what every cad deserves."

Having finished with the Sūfī, the Gardener
  devised a pretext of the same kind as before.

---

[1] Junayd of Baghdād, an eminent Sūfī, died in 911 A.D.
[2] See p. 100, note 1.

"My dear Sharīf," said he, "I have baked some scones for breakfast.

Will you go to the house and bid Qaymāz bring them to us along with the goose?"

Then, turning to the other, "Doctor," said he, " 'tis manifest and sure that thou art skilled in the law;

But thy friend a Sharīf! His claim is absurd. Who knows who committed adultery with his mother?

He has tacked himself on to 'Alī and the Prophet, and in the world there are plenty of fools to believe him."

He spoke plausibly, and the Jurist hearkened to him. Then that insolent bully went after the Sharīf.

"You ass!" he cried, "who invited you into this orchard? Is robbery your inheritance from the Prophet?

The lion's cub resembles the lion: in what respect do you resemble the Prophet? Tell me that!"

The Sharīf was devastated by the blows of that ruffian. He said to the Jurist, "I have got out of the water.

Now you are left alone. Stand fast! Be like a drum and take your beating!

If I am no Sharīf and unworthy of your friendship, at any rate I am no worse for you than such a ruffian as this."

The Gardener came up to the Jurist, saying, "What sort of jurist are you? The veriest fool would be ashamed of you.

Is it your legal opinion, O convicted thief, that you may come into my orchard without asking leave?

Have you read such a licence in the *Wasīt*, or is this question thus decided in the *Muhīt?*"

"You are right," he replied; "give me a drubbing! This is the fit punishment for one who deserts his friends."

L

THE MONK IN SEARCH OF
A MAN [1]

A MONK was seen in the daytime going round
   the bazaar with a lighted candle, his heart
   filled with love and rapture.
Some busybody said to him, "Hallo, what are
   you seeking in every shop?
What is it you are in search of, going round
   with a candle in the bright sunshine? What
   is the joke?"
He replied, "I am searching everywhere for a
   man who is made living by the life of the
   spirit.
Is there a man in existence?" "Why," said the
   other, "this bazaar is full of men, O noble
   sage."
The monk said, "I want one who is a man in
   the way of two passions—anger and lust.
Where is he who proves himself a man in the

---

[1] Book V, *v.* 2887. Diogenes Laertius in his *Lives of the
Philosophers* relates this Story of Diogenes the Cynic:
λύχνον μεθ' ἡμέραν ἅψας περιῄει λέγων "ἄνθρωπον
ζητῶ." Phaedrus tells it of Aesop.

hour of anger or lust? In quest of such a man
I am roaming from street to street.
Where in the world shall I find one who is a
man on these two occasions, that I may
sacrifice my life for him to-day?"

LI

THE ECSTASY OF BĀYAZĪD[1]

THAT venerable dervish, Bāyazīd, came to his
disciples and said, "Lo, I am God."

That master of mystic knowledge exclaimed
rapturously, "Hark, there is no god but I, so
worship me."

When the ecstasy had passed, they said to him
at dawn, "Thou saidest such and such, and
it is blasphemous."

He replied, "This time, if I make a scandal,
come on at once and plunge your knives into
me.

God is incorporeal, and I am in the body. Ye
must kill me if I say a thing like that."

Again he became intoxicated by the potent
flagon: these injunctions vanished from his
mind.

The dessert appeared: his reason became distraught. The dawn broke: his candle became useless.

Reason is like the prefect: when the Sultan
arrives, the helpless prefect creeps into a
corner.

[1] Book IV, v. 2102.

Reason is God's shadow: God is the Sun. How
   can the shadow resist His sun?

When a man is possessed by a spirit, the attributes of humanity disappear from him.

Whatsoever he says is really uttered by the
   spirit: the speaker on this side is controlled
   by one belonging to the other side.

A spirit hath such influence and rule: how much
   more powerful must be the Creator of that
   spirit!

If a pot-valiant fellow shed the blood of a
   fierce lion, you will say that the wine did it,
   not he;

And if he fashion words of pure gold, you will
   say that the wine has spoken them.

Wine can rouse such transports: hath not the
   Light of God that virtue and potency

To empty you entirely of self, so that you should
   be laid low and He should make the Word
   lofty within you?

Though the *Qur'ān* is from the lips of the
   Prophet—if anyone says God did not speak
   it, he is an infidel.

When the *Humā*[1] of selflessness took wing and
   soared, Bāyazīd began to repeat those ecs-
   tatic words.

The flood of bewilderment swept away his

[1] The lammergeier or bearded griffon.

reason: he spoke more strongly than he had spoken at first,

Saying, "Within my mantle there is naught but God: how long wilt thou seek Him on the earth or in heaven?"

The disciples, frenzied with horror, dashed their knives at his holy body.

Like the fanatics of Girdakūh,[1] they were ruthlessly stabbing their spiritual Director.

Everyone who plunged a dagger in the Shaykh made a gash in his own body.

There was no mark of a wound on the body of the Master, while the disciples were drowned in blood.

Whoever aimed a blow at his throat saw his own throat cut and perished miserably;

And whoever struck at his breast, his own breast was riven, and he became dead for ever;

And he that was acquainted with that spiritual emperor of high fortune and had not the heart to strike a heavy blow,

Half-knowledge tied his hand, so that he saved his life and only wounded himself.

When day dawned, the disciples were thinned: wails of lamentation arose from their house.

Thousands of men and women came to Bāyazīd,

---

[1] A stronghold of the terrible sect generally known as the Assassins.

saying, "O thou in whose single shirt the
two worlds are contained,

If this body of thine were human, it would have
been destroyed, like a human body, by the
daggers."

O you who stab the selfless ones with the sword,
you are stabbing yourself. Beware!

For the selfless one has passed away in God
and is safe: he is dwelling in safety for ever.

His form has passed away, and he has become
a mirror: naught is there but the image of
another face.

If you spit at it, you spit at your own face; and
if you strike at the mirror, you strike at yourself;

And if you see an ugly face in the mirror, 'tis
you; and if you see Jesus and Mary, 'tis you.

He is neither this nor that: he is pure and trans-
parent, he has placed your image before you.

Close thy lips, O my soul: though eloquence is
at thy command, do not breathe a word—
and God best knoweth the right way.